The Golden Valley

The Golden Valley

When Rossendale led the world

CHRIS ASPIN

First published in 2018
by Palatine Books,
Carnegie House,
Chatsworth Road
Lancaster LA1 4SL
www.palatinebooks.com
Copyright © Chris Aspin
All rights reserved
Unauthorised duplication contravenes existing laws
The right of Chris Aspin to be identified as the author of this work has been asserted in
accordance with the Copyright, Designs and Patents act 1988
British Library Cataloguing-in-Publication data
A catalogue record for this book is available from the British Library
ISBN 13: 978-1-910837-15-3
Designed and typeset by Carnegie Book Production
www.carnegiepublishing.co.uk

Printed and bound by Jellyfish Solutions

Contents

Introduction	vii
Self-made men	1
3,000 for tea	5
Working-class capitalists	8
Dividends for all	13
The Midas touch	18
Prosperity	22
The place to be	25
'The Slipper King'	28
The whisky spinners	34
The Blue Ribbon Army	48
The Opal of the West	54
A Bacup 'adventure'	61
The first IQ test	64
Electric shocks	66
'The Wonderful Telephone'	69
Flying boilers	75
A novel encounter	77
Runaway trains	79
Aerial adventures	81

Wheels of misfortune	84
Bravo Bottesini!	87
The Queen of Song	93
The musical mill master	96
'The pinnacle of fame'	100
Practice makes perfect	109
Arctic football	111
Gentlemen and players	115
The Hallelujah pig	124
A memorable trip	129
New heights	131
Index	134

Introduction

I HAVE WRITTEN ABOUT Rossendale enterprise since I first took an interest in local history as a teenager; and having updated and edited my numerous articles, I offer the story of the Valley's golden years in the nineteenth century. Because there was enormous self-confidence in those days and little outside interference, the transformation of the district was astonishingly rapid and attracted the admiration of people both in this country and abroad. Those who control our affairs today could learn much by studying our ancestors' achievements.

My thanks are due to the many people who have helped my research, and I am especially indebted to John Simpson for adding much of value to my stock of knowledge.

Chapter 1

SELF-MADE MEN

'DID YOU EVER HEAR of the Forest of Rossendale? You should visit the district,' says a character in Benjamin Disraeli's novel *Coningsby*, published in 1844. 'It is an area of twenty-four square miles. It was disforested in the early part of the sixteenth century, possessing at that time eighty inhabitants ... The eighty souls are now increased to upwards of 80,000 and the rental ... amounts to more than £50,000. 41,000 per cent. on the value in the reign of James I'.

Though the future Prime Minister overstated the population – it was about half that – he was clearly impressed by the Valley's reputation.

When Disraeli wrote his book, Rossendale was making enormous industrial progress, but its golden years were yet to come, for the second half of the nineteenth century saw the astonishing achievements of self-made men and the triumph of co-operation.

Several factors spurred this remarkable growth. Legislation was largely beneficial, rather than intrusive, and by reducing the long hours of factory work and allowing people to form their own joint-stock companies and co-operative mills, set the Valley on a prosperous course. The coming of the railway boosted trade; improved the diet of the inhabitants by allowing shopkeepers to stock fish, fruit and other perishable foods; brought job-seekers and visitors – entertainers, politicians, evangelists, lecturers, circuses – from all parts of the country; and through cheap travel, widened the horizons of many. Self-sufficiency bred independently-minded communities, which were protected from immoderate growth by noble hills and which were bound tightly together by the caring role of numerous organisations. In the small towns and villages from which Rossendale drew its strength, churches and chapels catered for many of the social as well as the religious needs of their adherents and most people took advantage of the opportunities that extra leisure afforded.

Almost all the money made by local enterprise was re-invested in the district, and this growing wealth boosted the wellbeing of a largely contented population, which believed progress would continue unabated. The masters built their mansions; the co-operators built mills and, along with several of the friendly societies, substantial houses that are still with us. The Haslingden Oddfellows were particularly active, building Numbers 331 to 349, Blackburn Road (near Acre) and the five houses of Mount Pleasant View in Bury Road. There, No. 91 has a date stone of 1869 and the initials of the National Independent Order. In the same year, the splendidly-named True United Sons of Adam erected eight houses in Grane Road.

By 1857, it was estimated that 2,790 Haslingden people – about one in three of the total – attended Sunday schools, 'a greater number in proportion to the population than any place in Lancashire'; and in the same year 'no place except Clitheroe sent so few criminals to the county jail'. Friendly societies and trade unions diminished distress; mechanics' institutions and co-operative societies (each with a library) stimulated learning; and choirs, orchestral societies and brass bands, some of which achieved national fame, made Rossendale a musical power in the provinces, as did the sports clubs which sprang up in every town and village.

Before the Ten Hours Act of 1847, 'it had been all bed and work', wrote Moses Heap (1824–1913), the local diarist, who was carried to a mill on his father's back at the age of five. 'Now, in place of 70 hours a week, we had 55 and we did not know how to pass our time. It became a practice, mostly on Saturdays, to play games, especially football and cricket, which had never been done before.'

Stone from the local quarries accounted for almost every new building – terraces for working people; mansions for the self-made men, who had accumulated enormous fortunes; churches whose architecture – plain or gothic – reflected the beliefs of their congregations; and public buildings, among which the workhouse opened at Pike Law in 1870 resembled, with its twin cupolas, more a potentate's palace than a place for the poor. By 1880, only one person out of every sixty two in the Haslingden Union was a pauper, compared with one in twenty nine for the whole of England and Wales. Ten years later the figure was one in 107.

Though hours of labour were long and sanitation in places deplorable, people made the most of their more agreeable surroundings. Beatrice Potter [Mrs Sidney Webb] who visited relatives in Bacup in the 1880s, found that the mill, the chapel and the co-operative store were the three things that dominated the lives of the working class; and she told her father, 'This is the only society I have ever lived in, in which religious faith really guides thought and action, and forms the basis for the whole life of the community. Class spirit hardly exists.'

Self-help, a firm belief that things could only get better and a strong companionship were evident, not only in the chapels and co-operative societies, but also – and often dramatically – in the support given to the sports clubs and brass bands which sprang up in every quarter of the Valley. When Irwell Springs Band won the national championship at the Crystal Palace on three occasions – the first to do so – thousands gathered in the main street to learn the result sent to Bacup by telegram; and almost every inhabitant left home to welcome the players on their return. Cup-winning cricket teams received a similar welcome.

Civic pride had taken root, and at a more local level it manifested itself in intense rivalry that surfaced when Haslingden, Bacup and Rawtenstall played one other at cricket. Rivalry also motivated the co-operators, each store and mill striving to outdo the others by paying the biggest dividends. Shareholders soon replaced managers who failed to take them to the top. Even the churches and chapels strove each year to collect the largest collection when the 'Sermons' Sunday came around.

Local newspapers – Tory and Liberal – which were launched in the 1860s, highlighted the conflicting views of a politically-minded population and stimulated local pride by covering events in great depth. Before their introduction people gained most of their news by word of mouth, from bellmen and from distant publications.

Rossendale became a Parliamentary Division in 1885 and attracted national attention in 1892, when John Henry Maden, a 28-year-old Bacup mill owner, whose grandparents had begun their married life in poverty, defeated the business leader Sir Thomas Brooks, of Crawshaw Hall, in one of the most important Parliamentary contests during the struggle for Irish home rule. Brooks was a Liberal Unionist: Maden, a Liberal, who supported Gladstone.

When, towards the end of the century, the three Valley towns became boroughs, they included in their coats of arms symbols of local enterprise – bales of cotton, a fleece, a shuttle, a block of stone, a cog wheel, a pickaxe and a spade. The accompanying mottoes emphasised hard work, and that of Rawtenstall – 'He prospers who labours' – gave the reason for the Valley's ascendancy. The district had gained a much-envied reputation, and the people who lived through the golden years had good reason to believe there was nowhere in Great Britain a more independent and progressive community.

Chapter 2

3,000 FOR TEA

IN MANY ROSSENDALE HOMES on the beautifully fine morning of 20 April 1861, excited families gathered up their cups and saucers, their knives and forks and their teapots and made their way to Cloughfold. It was the day of the great tea party arranged by the working-class co-operators who had built the five-storeyed Victoria Mill and who wished to mark their achievement in a memorable way. Some 3,000 shilling tickets had been sold, but as the *Bury Times* noted, 'Such was the demand that the committee could have disposed of a thousand more if there had been adequate accommodation.' Not surprisingly, 'Some persons who had a keen perception of the value of a good dividend, purchased tickets and resold them at a profit of fifty per cent.'

Along with the cutlery and the crockery came large quantities of food, including 1,196 lb of bread, 1,000 currant buns, 1,000 tea cakes, 380 lb of beef, 330 lb of ham, 344 lb of plum loaf, 300 lb of sugar, 220 lb of butter and much else. The tea was advertised for half past three, but long before that time, 'the highroads and footpaths in the locality presented a very animated appearance in consequence of so many persons assembling in a comparatively rural district. As everyone appeared to be decked in holiday attire, the scene was most attractive.'

The Newchurch Spinning and Weaving Company's mill, along with other co-operative ventures, helped to transform Rossendale into 'The Golden Valley' during the middle years of the nineteenth century. 'A very large and enthusiastic meeting at the Black Dog, Newchurch, on September 15, 1859, saw 200 shares of £10 each taken up within a matter of minutes and other subscribers took the rest of the capital during the next few days.'

Less than three months after its formation, the company began production at Vale Mill in Newchurch, the first piece woven being used as a tablecloth at the directors' Christmas party.

So brisk was the cotton trade and so great were the rewards that every Rossendalian who could scrape together a few pounds took a stake in it. Established companies expanded, bringing in people from as far off as East Anglia. The Newchurch co-operators joined enthusiastically in the headlong expansion by building Victoria Mill, which had the space for all the machinery needed to provide yarn for its 700 looms.

In February, 1861, the shareholders held their half-yearly meeting in the new mill, which pleased them so much that they the determined to celebrate their good fortune with the tea party, a public meeting and a ball for as many co-operators as possible. About 700 persons could dine at once, said the *Bury Times*. The 160 waiters or assistants had a busy time.

After the meal, the ticket-holders made their way to a large room on the second floor of the mill, where, as the newspaper put it, 'a feast of reason had been prepared for their delectation'. The walls were covered with crimson cloth, as was the large platform on which 'the splendid band of the Fourth Lancashire Rifle Volunteers performed some very beautiful selections'. There were songs by a Mrs Sunderland and a Mr Delavanti and 'Mr W. E.Spragg, of Bury, presided at the pianoforte'.

The public meeting began with the band playing the 'Hallelujah Chorus' after which the room became so full of 'conversation parties' that the speeches were heard only by those nearest the platform. At one point, things became so confused that after several attempts to obtain a hearing, 'the chairman sat down and a cornet was sounded to intimate that Mrs Sunderland was about to favour the audience with a song'. Order was obtained and Mrs Sunderland gave 'The Captive Greek Girl'.

One of the speakers, Frank Hunter, a Bacup accountant, advised the young ladies in the audience to ask their sweethearts how many shares they had in joint stock companies before accepting proposals of marriage.

> It has become an important question now, for almost every person who makes any claim to economical management in this district thinks of becoming a cotton proprietor; and the ladies generally are looking for husbands in the cotton trade.

Richard Hacking, of Bury, whose firm had built and installed the mill engine, said he had received orders worth £200,000 from co-operative mills, and he recalled that he had equipped the very first of them for the Bacup and Wardle company some eleven years earlier.

Chapter 3

WORKING-CLASS CAPITALISTS

DURING THE 1830S AND '40S, working-class reformers tried to persuade the Government to adopt 'The People's Charter', the main demand of which was a vote for every adult male. Though Chartism is usually dismissed as a failure, it was a starting point for other progressive movements, most notably co-operation, which enjoyed some of its greatest triumphs in Rossendale.

The Bacup Chartists opened a store in 1847; and having seen it succeed, decided that like-minded men and women should build and run their own factories. They began modestly, seventeen of them contributing half a crown towards the cost of promoting just such a venture. In 1850, they registered the Bacup and Wardle Commercial Company, which wove its first cloth in August of that year. The capital was £5,000, made up of 200 shares of £25 each. The office was in Temple Court, Bacup, and the weaving shed at Clough House, Wardle. James Hinchcliffe, whose father was a building contractor in Bacup, drew up the plans for the mill and was the first managing director. His obituary in the *Bacup and Rossendale News* of 22 May 1882, says the other directors were a warehouseman, two mechanics and a cotton weaver. 'When the mill was built and the looms "gated", there was no money to procure the wherewithal to set to work,' the notice adds. But a start was made; and at the beginning of 1851, the *Christian Socialist* carried the following note by its editor:

> We have just finished reading the deed of settlement of the Bacup Commercial Company, an association which has registered itself under the Joint Stock Companies Act. We had the great pleasure some days ago of visiting the admirably conducted mill belonging to the association, and we are therefore able to assure our readers that it is in practice an association of working men.

In October of that year, the journal described the mill as 'a fine building containing seventy two looms and worked by a twelve horse power engine'. There were fifty five employees and seventy shareholders, of whom thirteen or fourteen worked in the mill. The business was so successful that the pioneers decided to build a much bigger mill at Farholme in Stacksteads, and to spin as well as to weave. The expansion prompted a slight change of name: the New Bacup and Wardle Commercial Company was registered in February, 1854. The directors were Henry Clayton, a joiner; Joseph Greenwood, a spinner; John Howorth, a power-loom overlooker; John Pickup, a beamer; and Thomas Taylor, a carder. All had jobs in other Bacup mills. The trustee was James Carter, a wholesale grocer in Bacup.

The working men's mill, which wove its first pieces in August, 1854, astonished the cotton industry in 1859 and 1860 by paying successive half-yearly dividends of 31, 44 and 62½ per cent – an achievement no other company ever equalled. A correspondent of *The Co-operator*, who described Farholme in July, 1860, as one of the finest mills in Rossendale, commented:

> They tell us through the press and from the platform that we are too ignorant to manage our own affairs, but when the wealthy manufacturers begin to surpass the production of this mill, they may boast of their own abilities over those of the working class.

Success led to the mill's extension, and in 1860 three steam engines drove the machines. In that year, Captain Patrick, the locally-based factory inspector, reported:

> The large majority of shareholders are operatives who work in the factory, but receive wages as working men and have no more to do

with management than giving their votes at the annual election of the committee of management. I have been through the mill this morning and I can report that so far as the Factory Act is concerned, it is as well conducted as any in my division.

Farholme's achievements were noted as far away as Coventry, which sent a Mr Bracebridge to Lancashire to find mills willing to offer jobs to the city's unemployed. The notes of an unnamed diarist who accompanied the investigator appeared in the *Coventry Herald and Observer* on 26 July 1860.

> We went to Bacup, which is a large manufacturing place, although the mills and houses are much scattered. There are many co-operative mills here, that is mills in the hands of the operatives themselves. They select men from among their member to manage the business, and pay them one per cent of the profits.
>
> We examined two mills, which are not quite so good in their internal arrangements as those around Blackburn, but they were in a very healthy locality, and the people seemed healthy and cheerful. They are now in want of hands and have no objection to take a few families.
>
> We were introduced to no less than 17 manufacturers, who were assembled together. They heard our statements and behaved with great courtesy.
>
> Bacup is important, inasmuch as it is at the head of another large cotton manufacturing place called Rossendale. They are both bound together in an Association for the introduction of hands from all parts and have perfect arrangements made for their reception &c.
>
> At the various mills the books were shown us and we found that the average paid to the workpeople was as under –
>
> In mill A, the wages for weavers averages 19*s*. 9*d*. per week, after reducing 5*s*., the wages of a boy who assists the weaver.

> In mill B, the winders get an average of 10s. 6d. weekly, but this rate of payment is below that of the district generally, probably on account of some very young girls being employed. Warpers receive from 12s. to 14s. per week.
>
> In Mill C, the winders get from 13s. to 14s. per week and the warpers 16s. to 17s.

The company's success encouraged others. The Rossendale Industrial Association (subsequently the Rossendale Industrial Company) was formed at Weir in 1854, all its operatives being shareholders. A year later the Haslingden Commercial Company followed with a mill at Paghouse. When the Bacup and Wardle's huge dividends electrified the valley, all who were able became shareholders either in the existing mills or in those that followed. 'It is nothing uncommon here,' wrote a reader of the *Bacup Times*, 'to find a family transmuting comfort, pleasure, aye, even health and life into "Co-op" shares; to such an extent has the pursuit of wealth become a mania with us.'

Each big dividend from the new concerns produced a stampede for shares in every new venture, and when the Whitworth Manufacturing Company was formed at the end of 1860, a butcher and a clogger in the village along with a Rochdale boot and shoe dealer received applications in their shops. As a correspondent of *The Co-operator* noted in July, 1860:

> Here Co-operation is the only question which receives anything like support ... but it is in *manufacturing* that this district is causing most excitement. There are at present nine joint stock companies for spinning and weaving ... and there are in course of erection three mills besides the enlargement of others. These companies have a capital of £214,000.

'Bacup,' said a townsman in a letter to the *Rochdale Observer* at the end of 1860, 'is one of the richest and ablest places in Britain; nor is its wealth confined to the few, but is generally spread among the whole inhabitants.'

Do you notice that man in clogs and greasy corduroys? Would you believe me, sir, if I told you there goes a man of independent means, having his shares in this and that 'Co.', reaping in 'divi' his £2 or £3 weekly, independent of his own weekly wage as a three-loom weaver?

By now the path first trodden by the Bacup Chartists had led to a destination they could never have imagined, for many of the Rossendale mills were firmly in the hands of the workpeople.

Other new capitalists formed companies by inviting the public through newspaper advertisements to take up shares. The Haslingden Cotton Weaving and Spinning Company, formed in 1861, built Acre Mill.

It is interesting to reflect that while the new industrial revolution was accelerating in Rossendale and other places which put their trust in co-operation, Karl Marx was prophesying in *Das Kapital*, of 1867, that the rich would grow richer and that, as a consequence, more and more workers would sink into poverty.

In 1861, the New Bacup and Wardle Company's shares rose to a peak of £26 and seemed poised to rise still more when the outbreak of the American Civil War disrupted the supply of cotton to Lancashire, causing a severe crisis, which halted the growth of Rossendale for more than three years.

Chapter 4

Dividends for all

Rossendale suffered severely during the Cotton Famine, though less than districts which had yet to embrace co-operation. 'The dark hour has now come,' wrote the Bacup correspondent of the *Rochdale Observer* of 2 November 1861, in the first of many reports that told of mill closures, short-time working, soup kitchens and schools for the unemployed. When shareholders in the new companies were denied relief by the Poor Law Guardians, the Co-operative Relief Committee of the Haslingden Union, which included Accrington, received donations from John Stuart Mill and Richard Cobden, who told Henry Ashworth, his colleague in the Anti-Corn Law League, 'It is the most sorrowful aspect of the whole affair to see the very pick of the working class – those who were struggling for the emancipation and elevation of their class – thus struck down in the front rank by this terrible visitation'. In reporting the appeal, the *Bury Times* of 24 January 1863 commented:

> The growth of co-operative manufacturing companies on the limited liability principle has been very rapid. And the interest at stake may be judged by the fact that in the Haslingden Union seventeen of them exist with seven or eight thousand shareholders and with a paid up capital of £300,000.

The philanthropic Dr John Binns, of Haslingden, chairman of the relief committee, launched the appeal with a donation of £20.

Most of the companies survived the 'Famine' and co-operators who limited their interest to the retail stores were cushioned against the disaster. The Cawl Terrace Society, of Rawtenstall, actually increased its dividends every year throughout the crisis, and as one of its members said in 1865, 'By the aid of co-operation we have been living in the midst of distress in comparative comfort and pleasure.' At this time the Rossendale stores had more than 6,000 members, who, with their families, accounted for half the population. The founders looked back at their progress: the humblest of beginnings, several years of modest progress and then an almost unbelievable transformation.

In 1849, the Stacksteads society began in a cellar, where 'a tub the wrong way up' was used as the counter. A year later six men launched the Rawtenstall society with just 3s. 9d. The Water co-operators, in April, 1852, took a cellar at a low rent, borrowed an old table and bought some scales and weights, some wrapping paper and four lead pencils. Thus equipped, they began their quiet revolution. These and similar groups, by insisting on ready-money payments, destroyed the evil of credit trading, which had kept many working people in perpetual debt. Quarterly dividends replaced the shopkeeper's 'strap book', and, of equal importance, an end to the fear of injury and even death from adulterated food. Once established, the co-operative societies began to build substantial houses for their members and to open well-stocked reading rooms and libraries. By 1870, Bacupians were able to borrow microscopes, telescopes, opera glasses and other optical instruments.

A member of the Bacup store, looking back in 1876, recalled:

> The society had many difficulties to contend with. It was unpopular with the people in general and a certain section in particular. Some said it would quietly die a natural death, others that it would come to an untimely end. Some laughed at it; others sneered; and many thought it beneath their notice as the members were only a few Chartists. In spite of these predictions, the business kept steadily increasing. The members were able to obtain good food &c at a reasonable price and receive a round sum in the shape of a 'divi' four times a year. These advantages made a kind of civil commotion in the outer world. People began to see the result of the indomitable energy and perseverance of the pioneers, and numbers hastened to join the society.

With a good deal of trepidation, the promoters of the Haslingden Industrial Co-operative Society made their first sales in a cellar at the corner of Bury Road and Chapel Street in 1852, and fearing ridicule, they drew lots to decide who would open the shutters on the first night. Swift progress followed, however, and larger premises were soon needed. By the 1870s membership topped 1,200 and the dividend in 1874 was 2*s*. 6*d*. in the pound. The making and mending of clogs became a service at most branches and later growth saw the opening of a slaughterhouse, a bakery, tailoring and drapery shops and a furniture department. A butcher's cart toured the town to serve members at a distance.

Next came the building of rows of houses in Blackburn Road, Rock Street and at Longshoot, each with a store at its centre. The society also contributed importantly to the educational and social life of the district, opening a library and five news rooms, forming choirs, promoting lectures and giving annual tea parties attended by more than 1,000 members.

The management committee was kept on its by toes, not only by a strict disciplinary code – members were fined 1*s*. 10*d*. for telling tales outside the meeting room – but also by an elected group, which stood by the door to make sure there were no key-hole listeners. A box outside the room received complaints from members.

Another benefit was the reduction of drunkenness, 'Drinking is bad enough in Bacup, but the publicans' trade is decreased by 50 per cent by co-operation,' said *The Co-operator* in 1860. The society then had 1,350 members and a staff of 28. Like their colleagues in Haslingden, the Bacupians moved into bigger premises, the formal opening, on Good Friday in 1863, of a large store and meeting place attracting more than 2,000 members. The tea party which followed was said to have been the largest social gathering ever held in the town.

When the Rawtenstall society chose a site in Bank Street for a large new building in 1861, the architects were instructed 'to spare nothing in construction, but to economise on ornament'.

The opening of the Co-operative Hall took place on 27 November, 1869, and among those invited to the ceremony was John Stuart Mill. He was in France at the time, but he wrote a letter of congratulation: 'The prosperous condition of the society and the extension of the co-operative principle to mills as well as to stores in your district is highly gratifying.'

The huge building had a news room, library and an assembly room with space for 1,400 people. It was ideal for tea parties, said a visitor, who found on the upper floor a large gas-heated tin cistern 'from which tea is drawn in pipes into the large room, where there is a serving table upon which to place the urns'.

The society had 960 members and was making a profit of £1,000 a quarter. The quarterly dividend was 2s. 5¼d. for every pound spent.

Though one of the smaller societies, Tunstead enjoyed the greatest financial success. Trading began 1860 and at the end of the first quarter some 50 members were enjoying the benefits it provided. In 1871, by which time membership had risen to 410, it was paying dividends of 3s. 4d., equal to an annual return of two thirds of the money spent. At its tea party that year, the president of the Bacup Society said the progress of the Tunstead store was unparalleled in the history of co-operation; and speaking in more general terms, he went on:

> There are not 50,000 persons in any part of this happy land who possess so much wealth as we in Rossendale. Taking the Haslingden Union or taking a radius of six miles, there is half a million of money invested in co-operation.

A month later, the annual report of the Bacup Society concluded:

> The co-operators of Rossendale, of which our society is the parent, have to a great extent produced their own houses, stores, halls, news-rooms, libraries, and manufactories; and thereby has arisen in our neighbourhood one of the richest communities of working men in this country.

'No one will deny,' said the Rossendale historian Thomas Newbigging, in a speech to the Bacup society in 1886, 'that the co-operative movement has been the salvation of untold numbers of families.'

> It has kept poverty from many a working man's door. It has diminished pauperism. It has sown the seeds of independence

and self-respect in ground that might have remained fallow and uncultivated but for its influence; and it is a powerful instrument and advocate of progress, not only in preaching a daily and hourly sermon, but leading the way to its attainment.

Conformation of this came from a group of old Chartists, who were interviewed in Haslingden in 1892 by a special correspondent covering the Rossendale by-election for the *Daily News*.

> We Rossendale people have learned self-help in the co-op shop. Co-op shops have been our school; some of us had no other school. 'Co-op shop', in the Rossendale vernacular, means co-operative store. The co-op shop and its branches are the chief landmarks in these go-ahead, self-reliant, valorously Radical boroughs of Haslingden, Rawtenstall and Bacup. 'To the left o' co-shop', 'to reet o' co-shop', 'top o' street afore thou coomst to co-shop' are specimens of street directions an inquirer is sure to receive. Co-shops and divis are favourite words in the business vernacular of the Rossendale operative. Divis mean dividends. The co-shop was, as our friend remarked, a good school not only of thrift, but also of politics, because, as our friend put it, self-reliance has been the basis of both.

One of the group then related how a few men clubbed together to start the first store.

> The big corn dealer wouldn't sell them anything, so away they trudged ower t'hills yon to Todmorden. They bought what they wanted, carried their loads on their backs across t'hills, and when they come home, they divided the lot according to the subscriptions. You ought to see our co-shops now.

> 'I have been looking at them,' said I. 'The co-shop has been a good school, and no mistake'.

Though most co-operators supported the Liberal Party, some were members of Conservative societies, which operated on the same lines as their rivals. Rawtenstall had a Red store and a Blue store, as did, at an earlier period, the hamlet of Haslingden Grane.

Chapter 5

THE MIDAS TOUCH

THE ACUTE SHORTAGE OF COTTON during the American Civil War drove up the price of some grades by 500 per cent, but even when the 'Famine' was at its height, Thorn Mill at Water worked on. The bales continued to arrive, thanks to the unorthodox and uncharacteristic enterprise of the mill owner, George Haworth. Before 1861, he had been regarded as a retiring cautious businessman. But on the outbreak of the war he began to speculate on the Liverpool Cotton Exchange. 'He seemed to have the Midas touch,' said an obituary notice in 1879. 'While nearly every other mill in the district had either stopped or was working short time, Thorn Mill was fully employed. Probably no other Lancashire manufacturer ever made so much money in any three years as did Mr Haworth'. With some of his profits, he built Reedsholme Mill in 1864 and began production there in 1865, his entire workforce following him from Water.

Haworth, the grocer's son who ended his days in a mansion – Springside House at Crawshawbooth – was not alone in having the Midas touch. Dozens of Rossendale men turned cotton into gold by seizing the unprecedented opportunities afforded by an industry, which grew throughout the nineteenth century and which was the first to make the whole world its market.

Police Superintendent Robert Jarvis, who took charge of the Bacup and Rossendale Division in 1864, knew the mill owners well and was well pleased with his posting.

> Rossendale at that time had the reputation of being one of the wealthiest valleys in England. Nearly all the manufacturers were self-made men, whose education had been snatched in the few short hours they had to spare from toil, and whose good-natured qualities, backed by real English tenacity of purpose and dogged perseverance, put them into commanding positions. Yet as they 'got on' they kept their simplicity of character; there was no side about them; they were really good natured, hearty and breezy.

Like the co-operators, the mill masters often seemed surprised at the extent of their success. 'Here I stand, the master of 2,000 workpeople; and yet I started with nothing,' said Robert Munn in 1858. These are the words of a man whose story would have delighted Samuel Smiles. Few Rossendalians ever worked as hard as Munn and few enjoyed greater prosperity.

Munn was born at Holt Mill, Waterfoot, in 1800. Within two years of leaving school at the age of 15, he started a small spinning mill in Edenfield and 'put out' the yarn to hand loom weavers. By working sixteen hours a day, he was able, after six years, to buy Old Clough (Irwell Springs) Mill in Bacup. Munn also became a member of the family commission business, which his father had started in a Manchester cellar and he frequently rode the 20 miles to the city on horseback before breakfast.

In 1833, Munn built Stacksteads Mill; six years later he and his brother John, with whom he had gone into partnership, bought Irwell Mills in Bacup; in 1844 came Edgesideholme (Lolly) Mill and shortly after that Whitewell Vale. The partnership lasted until 1863, after which the brothers ran separate firms. Munn remained senior partner in the Manchester business until his death in 1876.

During the 1840s, Munn took a leading role in the Anti-Corn Law Movement. He had, however, no time for reformers who sought to reduce the working day in factories to ten hours, for, like many others, he believed that the final 'golden' hour produced the greatest profit. This is not to say that Munn did not care for his workers' welfare. His wish to see them educated led him to support the foundation of Mechanics' Institutes in both Bacup and Newchurch as well as the Literary Institute at Stacksteads. Munn rode hundreds of times to Haslingden to preside at the meetings of the Poor Law Guardians, remarking on his retirement in 1866, 'I believe we have behaved kindly to the poor. For the past 20 years I do not recollect that we have sent one family to the workhouse'.

When his daughter married in 1858, Munn invited his employees to his home at Heath Hill where, in a tent measuring 120 yards by 60 yards, some 900 people dined together on roast beef, mutton, ham and plum pudding. The guests danced to the music of the Bacup and Whitworth brass bands, played games – quoits, wheelbarrow and sack racing, climbing a pole for a leg of mutton – and sent up balloons. 'Occasionally,' reported the *Bury Times*, 'the whole party formed in procession headed by the brass bands; and we have seldom seen so large an assemblage of workpeople'. The health and well-dressed appearance of the merrymakers 'reflected much credit on their employers'. Munn told his guests, 'Forty years ago I had neither money nor men. What I have acquired has been by labour – and my workpeople have participated in my prosperity'.

John Maden, of Bacup, and the Whitehead brothers, of Rawtenstall, were other 'Cotton Lords' who began life with very little. Maden, who was born in 1800, wove woollen cloth on a hand loom as a boy, and he often recalled that when he married, he and his wife 'had not a pound to bless us with'. They had a bed and a table, but little else. Maden was 37 when he became a mill owner, but by the time of his death in 1869, he occupied a prominent position in the Rossendale trade, running Throstle, Spring Holme and Lee Mills as well as heading a cotton broking house in Liverpool. Maden's son Henry, who carried on these businesses, left £327,000 in 1890. Two years later, his grandson, John Henry Maden entered Parliament as the Liberal member for Rossendale.

Thomas, David and Peter Whitehead, the virtual founders of modern Rawtenstall, wove on hand looms before going into business at Balladenbrook in about 1815. They carded and spun waste cotton in a small water-powered mill and 'put out' the weft to cottage weavers. By 1824 they were able to build Higher Mill in Rawtenstall, one of the first in Rossendale to spin and weave by steam power. David Whitehead recorded his struggles in his diary, which shows that being a mill owner needed considerable fortitude in the early days of the century. Like Robert Munn at Bacup, the Whiteheads saw their power-looms destroyed by rioters in 1826 and their mills halted during the 'Plug Drawing' disturbances of 1842. An Army officer warned David Whitehead in 1826, 'There are nightly meetings in which they are laying a plot to burn your mill down and take your life'. After several anxious weeks, Government spies learned that the plot had been abandoned because no one would pledge himself to cut Whitehead's throat.

The brothers dissolved their partnership in 1855 in order to provide businesses for their sons. Thomas took Higher Mill, David Lower Mills, and Peter cash with which he built the huge Ilex Mill in Bacup Road.

Chapter 6

Prosperity

THE END OF THE AMERICAN CIVIL WAR prompted an upsurge of activity in the Rossendale mills, which lasted until the recession in the late 1870s. 'Let me give you an amusing instance of how trade was booming,' wrote Robert Jarvis of his time as the Valley police chief:

> I was Inspector of Weights and Measures in addition to my other duties, and on visiting the shops one day, I was told that an old woman who kept a small shop had received her first dividend from a co-operative mill, which had not been open very long. A neighbour, who was also a shareholder, had brought it for her. 'Howd yhor apron!' he ordered her, and threw the money into her lap. The old lady looked astonished and bewildered. 'Why, whatever hasta done?' she exclaimed. 'Aw didn't want mi brass back; aw nobbut wanted mi divi'. And she had only got her dividend. It amounted to 70 per cent.
>
> Just a little experience of my own. The rattle of machinery in a cotton mill near where I was used to grate on my ears until I bought a few shares in the concern. The dividend was 25 per cent. The machinery ceased to rattle; its music was as sweet as the Aeolian harp.

The dividends paid by the co-operative stores provided most of the capital for the new manufacturers, and, as a member of the

Haslingden society told Benjamin Jones, author of *Co-operative Production*, in 1890,

> It is rather a curious coincidence that the profits paid by our distributive society during the past twenty years almost amount to the combined capital of the companies in Haslingden.

The correspondent describes in some detail the three concerns that pre-dated the Cotton Famine: Hargreaves Street (1861), Haslingden Commercial (1855) and Laneside (1863).

> The directors are all of the operative class, such as weavers, clothlookers, mechanics &c., but do not work at the place at which they may be a director. The only interest that they represent on the board of directors is the capital invested.
>
> The workpeople are not necessarily shareholders, although many of them are; but this does not affect their liability to be discharged at any time, provided the work which they do is not satisfactory. They are treated by the manager as if they had no interest whatever in the place. Absolute power, so far as the workpeople are concerned, is placed in the manager's hands, and he is expected to produce a satisfactory financial result at the end of the half year.
>
> The directors meet once every week, at which meeting the manager reports the state of the cloth and yarn markets and any other matter which is of interest to the company, but I understand that as a rule, where a competent manager is in position, his suggestions for conducting the business of the company are seldom questioned. The accounts are made up every six months, and a general meeting of shareholders is held within a month of the time of making up the accounts. If the six months' working has been satisfactory, the meeting, as a rule, is very orderly and peaceful; if, however, the working has been unsatisfactory, the directors and manager have a rough time of it.
>
> There is a rivalry between the companies, which is very stimulating. All are engaged in making much the same class of goods and you

will readily see that, given even conditions, so far as capital and machinery go, it is then a question of good judgment and ability as to which makes the most profit for the shareholders.

The weavers are paid piece wages, according to a standard list prepared by the Weavers' Association, which, I believe, is now a powerful organisation.

When the Cotton Famine began, the Hargreaves Street and the Commercial companies each had between 300 and 400 looms. They made no profits while the crisis lasted and the value of £10 shares fell to as little as £2. With better times, the dividends returned, and during the last twenty years each of these companies has built up a reserve fund equal to the original share capital, out of which each shareholder was allotted one share for every share he was then holding. This in addition to paying substantial dividends to the shareholders during the time that the reserve funds were accumulating ... I know that a dividend as high as 15% has been declared; very often it has been 10%, and very seldom has it been less than 5%. The present market value of [Hargreaves Street] is between £15 and £16 per share, and this is equal to over £30 per share on the original £10 share.

We are very proud of the working men of Haslingden, and we have only to point to the results of the several undertakings to prove that the working classes are able to guide, supervise and bring to successful issues works raised by their combined capital.

Chapter 7

THE PLACE TO BE

When the Cotton Famine ended, people again flocked to Rossendale, seeking work and high wages. Before the crisis they had been recruited by agents sent into the agricultural districts by the mill owners; now hundreds came of their own accord. 'On Thursday,' said the *Bacup and Rossendale News* of 21 April 1866, 'more than 80 persons, particularly from Norfolk, arrived in Bacup. It would be better if we could get 800, when so many wheels now standing might be in motion.' Some ten years later, the *Bacup Times*, of 10 June 1876, reported:

> There is quite a colony in Rossendale of what are termed 'foreigners' – people from the Midland counties, in particular Cambridgeshire … Although there is a depression in the cotton trade and a strong possibility of the mills running short time, the cry is 'Still they come'. A few days ago, two widows, one with a family of ten children and another with 11 children arrived in search of work. Another man and his wife with two children walked the whole distance from Chatteris, below Peterboro' to Bacup and were six weeks performing the journey.

Haslingden, which attracted many Irish families displaced by the Potato Famine and land clearances, nurtured the young Michael Davitt, who became one his native country's greatest patriots.

'Cotton and co-operation have been going rapidly ahead of late,' said the *Bacup and Rossendale News* of 1 April 1871. 'All the mills are running full time and preparations are being made to open new ones.' The same newspaper, it its review of 1874, observed:

> The co-operative movement has made great progress during the year ... Mill after mill owned by private firms have been 'floated' as co-operative concerns and as a consequence the share-broking fraternity have had a lively time of it.

Members of the public wishing to buy and sell shares in the new companies used dealers from the working class, who set up informal stock exchanges in Bacup public houses as early as 1860. By 1874, the brokers had made enough money to build permanent headquarters in Rawtenstall. 'The object of the promoters,' said the *Bacup Times* of 18 July, 'is to have a place more select and where the baneful influence of the public house will not be felt'.

> It is a substantial building [later the Town Hall] with a numerous suite of rooms for refreshment, conversation, smoking and the general transaction of business. It will be fitted up with every modern improvement and will compare with any first-class hotel or gentleman's club.

In January, 1876, the *Preston Herald* reported that share dealings had begun 'on a scale little dreamed of by its most sanguine supporters'.

Not every company was quoted on the open market. A number of mills remained firmly in the hands of the operatives, who worked hard for their dividends as well as their wages and who invariably bequeathed their shares to their children.

The shares in one of the largest family concerns, Joshua Hoyle & Sons, also had a restricted circulation, for when the business became a limited company in 1873, the founder's sons, Isaac and Edward Hoyle, offered a quarter of the equity to their workpeople in one of the first schemes of its kind. The company employed 1,200 people at India, Beach, Newhallhey and Plantation Mills. A notice posted on 14 October read:

> To many of you it is known that the business of our firm has been attended with considerable prosperity. There is no diminution of that success. Our business continues to be satisfactory, and we think that our mutual interest would be promoted by drawing still closer those ties which have so happily existed between you and us. We therefore propose to submit a scheme of industrial partnership to you by which all persons employed in these works, without distinction of age or sex, may have the opportunity of holding a share or shares and so participating in the profits.

When an employee left, his or her shares were sold either to the company or to other workers.

Rossendale people did not confine their investments to local concerns or even to the numerous Lancashire mills, which sought support during the 1860s and '70s. Entrepreneurs of all kinds looked to 'The Golden Valley' for capital, among them the promoters of the Ormskirk Steam Corn Mills Company, the Yarmouth and Ventnor Railway, Tramway and Pier Company, the Buffalo Hide Horseshoe Company, of Manchester, and the Duchess of Westminster Silver and Lead Ore Company, of Holywell, Flintshire. From the United States came prospectuses for the Keokut and Kansas River Railway Company, of Missouri; the Burlington and Missouri River Railroad Company and the Sious and St Paul Railway Company. Land in America was also offered to Rossendalians, who were given the chance to buy European government securities through the good offices of Ferdinand Wolfskehl, of Frankfurt.

Chapter 8

'THE SLIPPER KING'

READERS OF THE *Boot and Shoes Trade Journal*, on opening the issue of 25 January 1896, found 21 consecutive pages, which described with unexpected raciness the achievements of Henry Whittaker Trickett, of Waterfoot, whose story is one of the great romances of industry. 'The Slipper King' delighted in bold gestures, and it was entirely in keeping with his business methods that he should place in the journal the largest advertisement the trade had ever seen.

Trickett, who was born in 1856, left school before he was eight to work from five in the morning until half past seven in the evening in a felt carpet mill. He trained as a block printer, but during the depression of 1881, became a traveller for one of the district's emerging slipper firms. He quickly realised the potential of the new industry and in 1883, at the age of 26, started his own business with two unskilled helpers. Trickett's first workshop was a single room in Carr Lane, Waterfoot, and the first slippers were purely functional: 'something to put tired feet into,' as one of his employees put it. Trickett took on four more helpers and despite several lean weeks, ended the first quarter with a profit of £18.

Lacking the money to employ a traveller, but having accumulated a large number of odd slippers, he hit on the idea of sending them to the leading footwear shop in every major town and city in Britain. He left the Post Office to decide who should receive his samples.

So successful was the venture that by the end of the first year the workforce had risen to 60. In 1889, Trickett bought for £1,100 – an old song, he called it – the empty Gaghills cotton mill at Waterfoot and quickly transformed it into the most prosperous workplace in Rossendale.

Slipper making began in the mid-1870s with John W. Rothwell and Samuel McLerie both claiming to have been the first to sew waste ends of felt into marketable footwear. McLerie got the idea from his sister, a Mrs Wylie, who had made slippers in a Scottish print works. Rothwell's inspiration came 'from seeing carters use rough felt slippers over their shoes when loading carts with cloth'. The first slippers were made just as the cotton industry was about to enter one of its more serious depressions. In July, 1879, Rossendale was said to have been in a worse state than in the Cotton Famine. Out of 100 mills, only six 'comparatively significant concerns' were working full time. Some thirty five were stopped and the rest averaged three and a half days a week. With a pool of unemployed workpeople to draw on, with empty mills available at knock-down prices and with untapped markets on all sides, the pioneers of the slipper trade made rapid progress. By 1900, some 18 firms employing a total of more than 3,000 people, had been established in the Valley. The largest by far was that of H. W. Trickett, for some account of which we have the giant advertisement of 1896.

The first thing the reader saw was a picture of a blackboard resting on an easel. Its message was, 'The following pages will tell you something you ought to know, if you don't already know it.' Overleaf was the statement: 'Trickett is the largest slipper manufacturer in the world.' The laconic style continued.

> Page 3 – In two hemispheres, in Europe, Asia, Africa, India and America, a household word is Trickett.

> Page 4 – Blacks, whites, mullatos, creoles and aborigines all wear Trickett's slippers.

Page 5 – Trickett's reputation has been gained by ceaseless energy and anxious attention to the wants of the public.

Page 6 – There is not a nook or crevice in the whole creation where Trickett's slippers are not worn.

Page 7 – Trickett produces from 40,000 to 50,000 pairs of slippers per week. All sorts, sizes and descriptions. Felt or leather, cashmere, carpet, wool, woven and embroidered.

Page 8 – Sand shoes in thousands. Leather or rubber soles; brown or white. 20 per cent cheaper than anybody else.

Page 9 – Trickett enables every man, woman and child to enjoy the comforts of neat, durable slippers at less cost than most people waste every day.

Page 10 – 17 million, 130 thousand pairs of Trickett's slippers made and sold in 12 years.

The picture of an eclipse was next to catch the eye. With it was the statement, 'Trickett outshines all competitors. For style, quality and value, Trickett's slippers eclipse all others.' Page 12 carried a cartoon and the words, 'Trickett's slippers for men and wives, girls and boys and little nippers. From 1½d. to 3s. a pair'. On Page 13, readers were reminded that '60,000 men were slain at Waterloo and misery wrought in a million homes'. In contrast, 'Trickett has saved as many lives and promoted peace and comfort, too'.

Page 15 had a portrait of the founder, below which was the caption, 'Mr Trickett gives instructions to his managers to use only the best materials, employs the most skilful workmen and charges them to see that every customer has his due'. Next came the 'Five points in Trickett's business: Unlimited capital, sound judgement, lengthy experience, firm discretion, honest dealing'. The Eiffel Tower came next with the information that 'it can be seen from twenty miles away', whereas 'Trickett's slippers can be see all over the world'. Page

17 carried a challenge: 'Trickett began business in 1883. Look at his progress and see if you can find his equal'. The firm's year-by-year expansion was indicated on the next page by rods of increasing length. The accompanying statement read, 'Sure and steady progress is a test of merit, a reward of enterprise, a monument of industry, a guarantee of good value, a sure sign of continued prosperity'.

Page 19 showed a man reading a newspaper on which were the words, 'Trickett makes personal inquiry into the requirements of foreign markets. His friends in the West Indies will also see him shortly'. Page 20 was headed, 'The dark spot in civilisation lightened. Trickett's slippers in the Transvaal'. Below was a picture of two explorers, one of whom remarks, 'This is an historical moment! We have reached a spot where no civilised being has ever penetrated. Let us rest in the shadow of yonder rock'. The final page shows them at the rock with the first explorer exclaiming, 'Sold again! That Trickett is always in front of us'. On the rock are the words, 'Advertisements in the Transvaal are Kruger's monopoly. This space is reserved for Trickett'.

In 1900, Trickett employed 1,000 people and was selling 72,000 pairs of slippers every week. A representative of the *Gentlemen's Journal* found the rooms at Gaghills 'large and lofty, flooded with light and clean, clear air and without a trace of dust; in short, an ideal factory'. The machinery and machinists worked with 'an exactness, perfection and quickness we have never seen equalled'. Trickett and his salesmen travelled the world, setting up depots in Paris, Hamburg, Bucharest, Capetown, Johannesburg, Cairo, and Kingston, Jamaica.

Trickett paid great attention to advertising, which was always lively and often humorous. A much-used picture was 'The Great Transformation Scene'. This depicted a long line of wild and domesticated animals rushing into a large steam-driven contraption, there to be instantly converted into high-class shoes and slippers. The picture underwent several changes to keep up with the times. One version shows Trickett, whip in hand, urging on his 'raw material' from a primitive airship.

In the 1890s and long before the advent of children's illustrated comic papers, Trickett issued a strip cartoon to interest the young in his footwear. A verse accompanied each illustration.

> Now children dear, come one and all,
> From little Nell to John so tall.
> This day to town we'll quickly go,
> For Trickett's slippers, don't you know.

That night, when the family had gone to bed.

> Two wicked men soon picked the lock.
> They wanted that choice slipper stock.

Help was at hand, however.

> A 'copper' watching round the town
> Chased those burglars up and down.

After their capture, everyone hurried into the streets.

> The people now came out to look.
> To fill it all would fill a book
> They call aloud with might and zest,
> 'Trickett's slippers are the best'.

'This is a selfish world,' said one of the firm's advertisements in the late 1890s, and it continued:

> The man who lags is dropped like a hot potato. We're aware of it, and not furnishing opportunities to the dropping process. No! We are stepping out resolutely and helping the drum major to lead the band. Right up in front, where we can hear the parson's faintest whisper, is where we want to sit. We keep posted, making the right shoes at the right time at the right price.

Trickett pioneered profit sharing and was among the first industrialists to introduce a training school, a refreshment room and medical care As well as paying high wages, he set up clubs in which staff could save for holidays or insure against sickness. Few of his workpeople sought jobs elsewhere, and the six men he took on in the first days of the venture were with him 30 years later. Gaghills was the first shoe factory run by electricity; and in 1902, Trickett became the first person in Rossendale to own a car.

Along with his business interests, Trickett found the time for religion and politics. He was a lifelong Baptist and made a point of sending his salesmen into the world at prayer meetings on Waterfoot Railway Station. He represented Waterfoot as a Liberal member of Rawtenstall Council, serving a record five terms as mayor. He was made a Freeman of Rawtenstall in 1907 and was knighted in 1909. Trickett died four years later, his mind teeming with ideas for even greater innovation. His estate was valued at £120,907.

Chapter 9

THE WHISKY SPINNERS

Though the industrious Rossendalians of the Victorian years learned how to make lots of money, their risk-taking enterprise occasionally outran morality, as can be learned from the stories of the farmers, who turned to the illicit distillation of whisky in Musbury, Grane and probably other remote spots, for it is unlikely all were detected. When Grane began to export water as well as whisky, the reservoir builders, who cleared the site of Calf Hey Mill, found a complete still in the engine bed.

With a ready market for their potent and untaxed brew, the whisky spinners built elaborate underground distilleries, devised ingenious ways of transporting the liquor to their customers and, with a few notable exceptions, of outwitting the Excise officers.

In the *Haslingden Observer*, of 30 April 1927, Mr W. H. Preston, a former Deputy Magistrates' Clerk, said when he left Haslingden in 1909, it was believed that a still was operating in the neighbourhood of Broadhead, but sufficient information could not be obtained to warrant a search being made. He described whisky making in these terms:

> The apparatus generally consisted of two large barrels, a large square tin with a vent hole in the top and a coil of copper tubing. The first barrel contained the ingredients for making the whisky – generally potatoes cut small with a supply of treacle, barm, sugar and water. After this had been allowed to stand for a few days

for fermentation, it was called 'wash'. The wash was then put into the tin container and the vent hole was connected to the 'worm' or copper coil, which was in a barrel of water with the end jutting out of the barrel. A big fire was started under the container. The resulting steam passed into the coil and condensed into a liquid – pure and simple whisky of ravishing strength. The makers never knew how to rectify it, but it answered its purpose and was very popular among quarrymen and other inhabitants.

Metal waistcoats, which held between two and three gallons, and a container concealed in a donkey's saddle were two methods used to transport the whisky, though in Grane, on occasion, it seems to have been carried openly to the quarries in four-gallon buckets.

Whisky spinning began to make news, though briefly at first, in the mid century. On 13 March 1850, the Haslingden magistrates fined three men, who had been tracked down by police and excise officers. The detectives had found a still in an old empty cottage belonging to John Wood, of Edgworth; and another at Doles in Haslingden township belonging to James Entwistle. Both men were fined £50. Also in court was Richard Schofield (otherwise Richard Taylor), who had a two-gallon bottle of illicit spirits in his weaving shed at the Old Factory in Grane. He had to pay £25. In October, Richard Hargreaves, a hand loom weaver of Grane, failed to conceal his still, alongside which were fifty gallons of wash and a gallon of illicit spirits. His lack of vigilance cost him £30 and the loss of his equipment.

Twice during the latter part of the decade, newspapers told their readers of large-scale skulduggery in Haslingden Grane, that astonished not only the public, but also the hardened excise men, who had come across nothing similar before.

The *Blackburn Standard*, of 15 April 1857, described how Sergeant Bousefield, 'having by some means or other obtained information that an illicit distillery was carried on to a large extent at a farm called Bentley House', called in Mr Westall, the Haslingden excise officer. As a result,

On last Friday week at night, Mr Heath, supervisor of excise, Blackburn, along with Mr Westall and Mr Thompson, officers of excise, Sergeant Bousefield and a few of his men, went and searched the house, which is occupied by a person named Jonathan Haworth. After searching for a considerable time, a subterranean passage was found leading into a dark room. In this room there was a fireplace sunk into the rock, and there were in the room two fermenting tubs, which would contain twenty gallons each, in which was a small quantity of wash, showing that the tubs had been in use recently. On the premises were found a still, 20lb of treacle and two gallons of unfermented wort and a small quantity of whisky in a bottle … Haworth was brought before Henry Slater, Esq., at Haslingden and convicted in the penalty of £30, in default of payment of which sum, he was committed for three calendar months with hard labour.

The heavy fine was only the first of Haworth's troubles, for as the *Standard* reported on 20 May, he was charged by Mr Ellis Heath, supervisor of the Inland Revenue in the Blackburn Division, with being the proprietor of an unlicensed still for the manufacture of illicit whisky. The report goes on:

Mr Clough, who appeared for the board of Inland Revenue, stated that this was one of the most compact and connected private distilleries which had been brought to light, at any rate in this neighbourhood; and but for the vigilance of the officers of the Board, it might have been carried on for a length of time without detection.

At eleven o'clock on the night of 3rd April, Mr Ellis Heath, accompanied by the officers, went to the house of the defendant, which is situated an unfrequented and isolated part of the township of Haslingden. On going into the house, the officers proceeded to a square weaving shop, but observed there nothing put a pair of looms. On examining the room above that they found it was a very much larger room. The descended again to the weaving shop and tapped the wall, which the defendant said was the gable end of the house. They found the mortar soft, yet it corresponded with the other walls of the chamber. On looking at the flags they found that they had only been freshly laid. A few were taken up, and after taking up a quantity of earth, an arched entrance cut out of the solid rock was discovered with an aperture just sufficient for one person to enter in a creeping position. On the officers entering the chamber by this, the only entrance, they found a new still and every apparatus requisite for the manufacture of illicit spirits, with a number of tubs, a quantity of wash, &c, &c, which were immediately seized and conveyed to a place of safety.

The flue of the fireplace had been cut out of the rock and taken before the floor of the weaving shop and house until a junction was formed with the chimney of the house, so that the flue only could be seen to emit smoke. With the stone cut from the flue the partition wall of the weaving shop had been built so that no material had to be brought to the house.

Mr Ellis Heath and others proved the case and the bench inflicted a mitigated penalty of £50 and costs, in default of payment to be imprisoned during her Majesty's pleasure.

On the 7th ult., the defendant had been convicted of being on the premises where illicit was found, and convicted in £30 and costs, in default to go to prison for three months.

The prisoner then sold ten head of cattle and went to prison. The seizure reflects great credit on the vigilance of the officers and will do much to check illicit distillation in this district.

In the following year, the newspapers told an even more astonishing story. 'One of the most extraordinary cases of illicit distilling which ever occurred in this district was heard before the Blackburn bench on Saturday last,' reported the *Preston Guardian* of 4 September.

The offender, James Morris, resides at Pike Law, in Haslingden, and is the owner of a small farm, on which he resided and constructed his singular and subterraneous distillery. He is, we regret to say, a reputed religious character, and so far did he carry his infamous hypocrisy that he engaged in reading the Bible while the excise officers were endeavouring to discover where he carried on his illicit trade, he at the same time asserting his entire innocence of the transaction.

Mr Heath, the supervisor of excise, the report goes, said that from information he had received at various times, he went to farm in the previous February, but in spite of 'a very minute search of the house', there was 'no appearance of any illicit traffic being carried on'.

However, he was satisfied that the prisoner had carried on his lawless traffic to a very considerable extent. It was decided to make a powerful descent on the premises; and accordingly, on Wednesday last, excise officers from Haslingden and Blackburn, aided by some members of the county constabulary, visited the place. On arriving at the spot, and being unable to find anything externally, they resolved to employ the services of some spademen, who were called in for the purpose of digging all about the premises. The prisoner had a very nice little farm, which was his own and upon which he milked seven or eight cows. He therefore could not plead poverty in mitigation of his offence. He must have carried on his fraud upon the revenue to a very considerable extent extending over very many years, as the manufactory must have been constructed when the house was built.

The spademen 'worked with unabated energy' during the whole of Wednesday, and it was not until very late at night that they discovered a leaden pipe that brought water from a well across meadow, for rather more than one hundred yards.

They found that the pipe was laid in the direction of a building, but owing to the lateness and consequent darkness of the night on Wednesday, they were obliged to cease working. However a policeman was left in charge of the premises, and on Thursday morning operations were resumed with renewed energy. [The diggers] took much trouble to get to the termination of the pipe, which they did by removing all the surperincumbent earth. Thus the whole of Thursday and part of Thursday night was occupied, but they did not discover the fountain head. A policeman was again left upon the premises. On Friday morning the digging was suspended and the course of the pipe was traced by a long pole. Between twelve and one o'clock the pipe was traced to a certain place, next to which there was a turf room – full of turf.

Four or five loads were taken out of that place, and eventually Mr Mitchell found a small hole, about two feet in diameter, On entering this door, he found it led to a subterranean passage, which was discovered to be a tramroad used for the purpose of running articles from the entrance of the manufactory to the still. On proceeding to the end of the dark passage, which was discovered to be a tramroad used for running articles from the entrance of the manufactory to the still. At the end of the passage, he found a very extensive still, two large vessels of a peculiar shape, which were full of spent wash, fifty or sixty gallons. There also three large tin worms of considerable size. He understood the prisoner was a tinner by trade. All these implements had been made on the premises, and in the precise spot where they were found. They destroyed those and then and brought them away piecemeal, as the cavity was too small to allow of the utensils being brought away in their entirety. They brought the prisoner with them to Blackburn late on the previous night. They also brought away from eight to ten gallons of spirits of a very superior quality. On the premises were found funnels, cans, measures and every other appliance for carrying on a wholesale system of illicit distillation.

When the search party arrived, Heath, continued, Morris drove away his cattle, which he either disposed of or 'conveyed away in order to avoid an execution'. He frequently took down his Bible from a shelf 'and attentively perused its pages. He had always been known in his own neighbourhood as a man of strong religious professions'.

John Mitchell, an excise officer described how he and a policeman dug up the floor of the turf room and came across a sharp stone that appeared to form part of the top of an archway. The next lifted another flag and saw a small underneath.

> One of the flags was inserted in the wall. After removing that flag they found another placed upon a truck that ran upon four wheels. They found another aperture, which was less than two feet wide. The aperture gradually extended until it became two feet six inches wide, On pursuing the passage he found that it terminated abruptly, and on getting to the edge of it he suspended himself. He called to one of the policemen for a light. On one being brought, he found there was a perpendicular descent of from six to eight feet. He descended and followed that passage, but found nothing but some empty barrels. At the end of the passage he found a little door; its circumference was about three feet by two feet. On opening that door he found another passage, about eight feet long and of the same dimensions as the door at the entrance. On going through that passage, he found another, which led to a square cave that had no light in it. The cave was about six yards square and it he found three tin cans which held about forty gallons. They were all full of water. There were also three wooden tubs, which would hold from 100 to 110 gallons of water; one of them was sunk into the ground, and it was full of water. There was also a still on a furnace; the fire was laid but not lighted. They found five jars, two of which were full of whisky. Other jars contained whisky, but they were not full. On examining the dimensions of the place, he found it would be impossible to remove the utensils in the state they then were. He broke them to pieces and brought the pieces away with him. He was quite confident that the vessels had been made inside the cave.

Heath then told the magistrates that Morris was present all the time and was asked to show them the place to save them further trouble.

He had told them there was no point in searching as 'there was nothing of the sort about the place'. Asked how he pleaded, Morris replied 'Nobbut guilty'. Then, said the *Guardian*, he addressed the chairman [Daniel Thwaites, founder of the Blackburn brewing company] in a subdued and pathetic strain and 'hoped God would put it into his heart to be as merciful to him as he (God) was powerful, for the sake of all his little children that he had left behind him at home'.

> In reply to Mr Thwaites, the prisoner said that the farm upon which he lived was rather short of fourteen acres, and that it was partly his own; that he had had distemper in his cattle last winter but one and he had to get fresh ones as he could.
>
> Mr Thwaites told the prisoner that he had carried on an illegal traffic at the expense of the fair trader; that he had used much deception and had put the officers to much unnecessary trouble.

When Morris refused to pay the £30 fine, he was taken to Preston House of Correction to serve three months with hard labour.

The trial was not the end of the matter; and before the month was out, Morris was in court again, this time at Haslingden, where Heath, the excise officer, said he believed the Inland Revenue had been defrauded out of £700 a year. The report in the *Blackburn Standard*, of 29 September went on:

> [Heath] said he had communicated with the Board in London and they had ordered him to press for the highest penalty. He had no doubt but that the place had been built on purpose and that illicit manufacture had been carried on for fifty years. There was a drainer in the place which fitted so tight that not a particle of steam could escape. He had never seen such a place in al his experience.
>
> At one place they came to a long flag which they had taken up, expecting that they were going to find the entrance to another passage, but when the stone was taken up, mortar was found underneath and had all the appearance of being right. One policeman, more suspicious than the rest, thought there was more

in the stone being there than they imagined and put his hand upon the mortar, when something moved. The hand was again applied and the flag ran upon a railway on one side and left open a man-hole. The stone was so nicely adjusted that the least push would throw it on one side, and it would immediately return to its place as if nothing had been disturbed.

Mr Heath said he had no doubt in his own mind that the prisoner had gone down by the trap while they were searching the premises, and it was then that he cut the two worms into a hundred pieces. While they were searching, the prisoner, after driving out the cows, took down his Bible and in the presence of the officers read several chapters.

The magistrates said they would inflict the highest penalty, namely £200. The hypocrite will have to remain in prison during her Majesty's pleasure.

Research by John Simpson shows that the distillery was at Far Pike Lowe, which Morris's great-uncle William, a Bury hatter, bought for £360 in 1803. William's only brother John (a shoemaker, according to his will) inherited the estate; and on his death in 1826, each of his four children received a quarter share. William, the elder son, acquired the farm, which he worked until his death in 1849. The property then passed to Sarah, his widow, who lived until 1860.

James Morris, one of William and Sarah's seven children, was baptised at Blackburn in 1811 and died in Haslingden in 1874. The 1851 Census lists him as a handloom weaver living at Pike Lowe.

If we accept the Excise officer's statement that the distillery had been used for fifty years – from about 1808 – we must think of the business as a family or even a co-operative enterprise, for production on the scale described in court could hardly have been concealed from relatives and local people or, indeed, been carried out by one man, who in 1858 had also to look after the livestock on his twenty five-acre farm. Raw materials and fuel had to be bought, the whisky distilled and numerous customers secretly supplied.

After serving his prison sentence, Morris moved to Peak in Grane and at the time of the 1861 Census was a cotton engine feeder. It is reasonable to assume that he worked in Calf Hey Mill, where, interestingly, a still was found when the building was demolished.

Since I am speculating, let me suggest that the Bible-reading Morris was a Wesleyan Methodist who attended Grane Chapel, which opened in 1815, and which was the only place of worship in the district until St Stephen's was built in 1868. Morris's sister Mary was baptised at King Street Methodist Chapel in Haslingden in 1809, and she and her husband were buried in the Wesleyan graveyard at Grane. Did illicit whisky profits advance the Methodist cause?

Were Morris and Haworth rivals? Major Halstead in his *Annals of Haslingden* says that when the Excisemen were about to leave Morris's farm empty-handed, 'Mrs Haworth suggested they should go to a well and follow the pipe that led from there'. John Simpson found that Mrs Haworth (*née* Alice Holden) was the wife of Jonathan, the Bentley House whisky spinner. Her motive for ensnaring Morris is unclear, but Halstead states that 'The neighbours would never afterwards associate with the woman who gave the information'. The loss of an important industry may well have impoverished them as the following stories from Halstead's *Annals* would seem to show.

> Henry Hargreaves once told me that in his boyhood days he employed many handloom weavers. 'We found both warps and weft, for they did their work in their homes. We had a certain day for the cloth to be brought in, but there was one girl who came at all times except the right one and I finally told her I would make her take her piece home if she did not obey the order. She came again on the wrong day and I refused to take the cloth. She pleaded with me and finally she told me she could only bring the cloth when she was bringing whisky to a certain hotel in the town.
>
> 'I told her I didn't believe her. She asked me to come downstairs and she would show me the apparatus. She always came with a donkey, which carried the finished cloth thrown across the saddle. I went down. She lifted up the saddle and to my surprise there

beneath it was a hollow metal case, which was the size and shape of the saddle and which she said would hold three or four gallons.

The girl told me she had passed the Excise officer on her way and he had bid her a hearty "Good morning" as she rode past him seated on top of the piece on the donkey's back.

Her father knew that the Excise man suspected him, but up to then there had never been suspicion that the girl was the go-between the distiller and the publican.

Henry Taylor told me that when the Bury and District Water Board took out the steam engine on the demolition of Calf Hey Mill when building the reservoir, a complete still and all accessories were found in the engine bed.

An old resident of Grane told me that he had heard his father say that whisky did not cost sixpence a gallon to make. He remembered whisky being taken to the Grane quarries in four-gallon buckets.

The 1851 Census shows that Jonathan Haworth, who came from a farming family, was a cotton power loom weaver and was living at Ormerods in Grane, but he moved house at least four times after his prison sentence. He died in 1894.

Richard Hargreaves appeared before the Haslingden magistrates again some eight years after losing his illicit still. He was now living in a house at Ally Cross, on which Ellis Heath and his men swooped 'during the hours of divine service'. There, as the *Blackburn Standard*, of 24 February 1858 reported, they 'found Hargreaves and three or four others seated round the fire and smoking their pipes with a jug of illicit whisky and sugar on the table'. He was fined £25 and costs.

The *Standard*, of 4 August 1858, told of a farmer living at Yate and Pickup Bank – 'a reputed teetotaller and religious man' – who had been fined £50 at Haslingden for being in possession of five bottles of illicit whisky. 'The prisoner said he bought the whisky from an old woman that he did not know and used it to rub his arms for rheumatism, having been told that it would do him good'.

If the farmer had a hidden still, the detectives failed to find it, but others had no such luck. 'Discovery of a subterranean distillery' was the headline in the *Blackburn Standard* of 22 August 1851, describing the downfall of William Bromoley, a farmer at Brown Hill, above New Hall in Edenfield. The raiding party found the still in a cave, the mouth of which was covered by a flag.

Benjamin Westall, an Inland Revenue officer, told Haslingden magistrates that he and two policemen went down into the cave, which measured about three and a half yards by three yards, by a flight of stone steps. They found a still, still head, condenser, condensing tub, four fermenting tubs containing about seventy gallons of wash, a wooden pail which seemed to have been used for charging the still, a funnel, a milk can and other articles, all of which seemed to have been recently used. There was a small fireplace in one corner of the cave, and the still was on the top of the fireplace.

'The smoke,' said the witness, 'escaped through a sort of drain about four yards long. There was a stovepipe which fitted into an aperture at the end of the drain. This aperture was covered with a sod when the still was not at work. The stovepipe would stand about a yard above the ground when it was fixed. I would say the cave had existed from six to twelve months. It must have taken a man nearly a fortnight to make the cave.'

Policeman Green said there was about a hundredweight of coal in the cave, and the bars of the fireplace were nearly burnt through, apparently with long usage. The stone which covered the cave was about five feet long and supported by planks. The policemen destroyed the cave 'as far as possible'.

Bromoley was fined £50 and costs.

In spite of these heavy fines and the imprisonment of those who refused to pay, whisky spinning continued. It was clearly worth the risk.

In July, 1881, the *Blackburn Times* described how James Barlow, who had a small farm at Hare Clough in the Musbury Valley at Helmshore, was caught red-handed.

Haslingden policemen surrounded the property 'between one and two o'clock on Tuesday morning [7 July] and found a whisky still, complete and ready for use,' says the report. 'There was also a quantity of wash, barrels &c, all of which was seized. Later on in the day, a cart was obtained and the still, together with the liquor, barrels &c, was conveyed to the county police office at Haslingden, pending proceedings being taken by the Inland Revenue, who have been informed of the seizure, which has caused much excitement in Helmshore.'

> At the court hearing, a policeman stated that the still was built into a fireplace and that the water was piped from another room. The officers found a barrel and a tub, each of which contained about eighteen gallons of wash. A can in front of the discharge pipe of the condenser was full of whisky. The cellar was six inches deep in refuse from the still. Barlow was fined £10.

The Musbury Valley was in the news again in 1884, when several newspapers reported the discovery of a still at Ferny Bank. Two teams of policemen and excise officers, 'who were aware that quantities of whisky were being made in the district', carried out raids during the night of 7 March.

Henry Haworth, who was arrested, owned three farms – Lower Houses (in which he lived), Higher Hare Clough and Ferny Bank. His home yielded only a two-gallon bottle; the second farm had nothing, but at the unoccupied Ferny Bank one of the raiding parties 'discovered a complete apparatus for distilling whisky'. 'The occupier of Higher Hare Clough hinted that he knew some stills that were three miles away, but refused further information.'

'For many years,' said the *Manchester Courier*, 'illicit stills have been used in the district, the offenders finding a ready sale for the spirits they condense.'

At the court hearing at Haslingden, the magistrates were told that 'stairs at Ferny Bank were blocked up in various places, so that searchers, to get from one room to another, had to creep through holes, one of which was in a hayrick'.

Haworth was fined £30.

Though this was the last case of its kind, it is likely that other whisky spinners escaped prosecution; and Dr G. H. Tupling, the Rossendale historian, was told that Alice Entwistle, who had a still at Top o' th' Hillock in the 1860s, outwitted the police and excise officers when they searched her farm.

Chapter 10

The Blue Ribbon Army

TEMPERANCE IS AN UNLIKELY SOURCE of public excitement. Seen, however, as a crusade against the devastating evils of drink, it became for thousands of Rossendalians in the 1880s a passion which at times induced an intoxication almost as strong as that caused by alcohol itself. The Blue Ribbon Army has long been forgotten, but the battles it fought dominated life in every town and village for more than two years and had a restraining influence on succeeding generations. The campaign began in Haslingden in November, 1881, and met with instant success. 'Such a movement was never witnessed before. It came upon us like a wave with irresistible force,' said R. J. C. Mitchell, the Waterfoot felt manufacturer, who took up the cause with enthusiasm, though he had previously regarded temperance unworthy of serious discussion.

In spite of the obvious and tremendous misery which the abuse of strong drink was causing, its opponents in the Valley were poorly supported until the American, Thomas E. Murphy, began a fortnight's 'mission' as the guest of the Haslingden Temperance Society. His oratory, his use of rousing songs and his invitation to reformed drunkards to tell their stories, packed the Public Hall each evening. From the outset he gained the support of the churches, to such an extent on one occasion that the platform collapsed under the weight of 200 religious leaders, including the vicar.

The undoubted 'star' among the local reprobates anxious to confess their sins, was 'Bury Bob' (Robert Hamer), who gained national notoriety for himself and Bacup by fighting a bulldog in the Hargreaves Arms at Stacksteads. The encounter, though much exaggerated, was the subject of a question in the House of Commons and a lurid sketch in the *Illustrated Police News*.

According to the *Bacup Times*, of 5 March 1881, 'the 'big, burly and ferocious-looking' Hamer worried and ate rats and 'occasionally tries his teeth on pots and plates'.

> To him, 'cow-heel bones' are as ordinary food. Not long ago he chewed and swallowed a 'tot glass' in a well-frequented tap-room – the circumstance forming an interesting subject for several of the younger members of the medical profession.

Hamer tackled the dog after the owner 'under the influence of liquor and in a talkative mood' offered to back it against him. In the brief struggle, the account goes on, Hamer seized the brute by its right ear with his powerful teeth, pinned it to the floor and 'worried' it in such a manner that its boasting master 'threw in the sponge'.

The report, as the *Times* observed in its next issue, caused a sensation in all parts of the country. The *Bacup and Rossendale News*, having missed the scoop, accused its rival of 'journalistic prostitution' and called the story a gross exaggeration. It admitted, however, that Hamer seized the dog with his teeth, but that the battle was one-sided and did not last more than a minute and a half and no bets were made. The *Times* stuck by its story, but criticised other newspapers for embellishing the facts.

The police and the Royal Humane Society investigated the event as a result of which the Home Secretary was able to tell Parliament that the Chief Constable of Lancashire had assured him the whole story was 'a ridiculous exaggeration' and he did not intend to strengthen the police presence in Stacksteads, as one MP had suggested.

Hamer was not long out of the news, for when the Blue Ribbon Army marched into Rossendale, he was one of its first recruits. Not surprisingly, he topped the bill when he made his début as a public speaker at the Co-operative Hall in Rawtenstall in July, 1882. The *Times*, which had been so unflattering a year before, adjusted its description of him.

> 'Bury Bob' is a tall, dark swarthy man, about 35 years of age, with piercing eyes and close-cropped hair. He is not the coarse, brutal fellow one would expect to see. He possesses more than the average amount of intelligence and common sense. He addressed the meeting for about 15 to 20 minutes in a very creditable style.

Hamer's 'conversion from the error of his ways', as the newspaper so rightly observed, was 'a most remarkable victory' for the teetotallers, who paraded him throughout their campaign. He grew more confident as the weeks went by, but even on his first appearance, he had his listeners of the edge of their seats.

> He told the meeting that he had been bad in his day, but intended to try a new course in life. He had lived to serve the landlords long enough. Drink had caused him to part from his wife, broken up his home and injured his constitution in such a manner that he would never be able to recover his former health. He had been in prison 26 times and had done all kinds of horrid things for the sake of drink. For pints of beer he had swallowed 26 pocket knives, 15 of which remained undigested. He was told that if he continued to drink, he would not be able to rid his system of those 15. Well, in place of beer he would try what good food would do.

Hamer then attacked the 'selfish and hard-hearted publicans' who would take the last penny a man had even when they knew that his family would be without food during the following week. 'I know publicans who provide broth and suet puddings on Sunday for their customers, but none for the wives and children starving at home'. This was rousing stuff and wonderful ammunition for the Blue Ribbon Army. Overnight 'Bury Bob' became a temperance celebrity. When he spoke at the Bacup rally in August, 'he seemed to be the admired of all admirers,' said the *Times*.

> His rising was a signal for a general rush from all parts of the field towards the platform from which he spoke. He is possessed of a sonorous voice which made itself heard to the majority of the vast crowd which confronted him. His self-possession was amazing, and as he proceeded with his remarks, he astonished his hearers by his genuine natural wit and oratorical talent.

'Bury Bob' often referred to his past skill as a knife disposer. If they went to Lee Mill, the *Times* reported him as saying on 26 August, they might ascertain for themselves that, for the sake of a drink, he had swallowed five knives at one time'. What became of them he never disclosed.

At the end of its first fortnight in the town, well over 6,000 people – more than a third of the population – had signed the pledge. Not since 10 December 1857, when the Bacup teetotallers attracted 1,000 townsfolk to the Mechanics' Institution for a free helping from a 120lb barley pudding – the aim was to prove that barley was intended to be eaten and not drunk – had the Rossendale temperance cause received such a fillip. But this was only the beginning.

In December, 1881, 'a party of skirmishers' from Haslingden, aided by Murphy and his son Francis, took the war into Rawtenstall. Within a month, some 3,000 inhabitants were wearing the blue ribbon. Bacup watched the campaign with the greatest interest and in February, 1882, the Sunday school teachers met to discuss the possibility of engaging the charismatic American.

> Bacup, ever confident of her own abilities [said the *Times*] decided that Mr Murphy should not fill his pocket with the earnings of his sons. They would have a mission, but they would conduct it themselves.

Even without Murphy, abstinence was achieved on a huge scale. By May, the Blue Ribbon Army had more than 4,000 new recruits and 'scores of young men and others' were said by the *Times* to be flocking night after night to temperance meetings instead of going straight from work to the public houses. By the late summer, the number of teetotallers in the town had risen to 6,000, most of whom took part on 12 August in a procession which was followed by a rally requiring two large fields at Thorn. 'Newchurch Road and Market Street were one mass of people, the great majority wearing the blue ribbon,' the *Times* reported.

Meanwhile, in other parts of the Valley, temperance crusaders carried all before them. So full had the Sunday schools in Rawtenstall become by July that the Wesleyan Methodists were obliged to build an iron mission hall at Springside.

Though the movement had strong religious overtones, its organisers fully appreciated the value of secular attractions such as clubs, coffee taverns, social evenings, field days and (at Haslingden) a brass band. Very popular were the 'free and easy' gatherings held each Saturday evening in the Co-operative Hall in Bank Street, Rawtenstall. A visitor in April, 1882, found a 'plentiful supply of milk, buns and oranges' for the 'mixed multitude' who joined in the singing and listened to the addresses given by reformed drunkards and the advocates of temperance. There were also games, 'that which appeared to be most in favour' being one involving 'a great deal of kissing by both married men and single alike with much apparent enjoyment. The young ladies who happened to have the nicest-looking faces' not surprisingly 'received the largest share of attention'. No wonder the hall was always full; but here the writer entered an objection. 'Any young woman who can stand up in the face of 600 or 700 people in the public assembly and permit herself to be kissed and cuddled without feeling a sense of shame is to be pitied, and we would not like to say much in favour of her modesty'.

On 5 August 1882, some 2,500 people accompanied by four bands went to Rye Hill Haslingden, for a gala at which 'Teetotal Samson performed astonishing feats of strength with 56lb weights and allowed a large stone to be broken on his chest'. A firework display in the evening 'eclipsed anything of its kind ever witnessed in the locality'.

A procession through the streets of Crawshawbooth on the previous Saturday 'was the most imposing ever remembered by the oldest inhabitants,' wrote the *Times* correspondent, who counted

1,927 marchers. Though only six months old, the village mission had been 'crowded with success almost beyond the hopes of the most sanguine, some of the most drunken and dissipated having been reclaimed'.

As the number of teetotallers rose, the pressure on the police and the courts fell, and by the end of 1882, the clerk to the Haslingden magistrates was getting through his work in two days instead of the six he had needed when drunkenness was rife. The Post Office Savings Bank in the town saw the number of deposits rise from about twelve a week when the campaign began to almost 500, a reflection of the fact that more than 8,000 inhabitants had signed the pledge. The Haslingden v Bacup cricket match at Bentgate, traditionally the scene of fierce partisanship, passed off in 1882 'with a comparative absence of rowdyism,' a circumstance attributed by the newspapers to effects of the Blue Ribbon movement.

Very few abstainers gave way to temptation while the campaign lasted. One backslider was soon made to feel an outcast. He lived at Hugh Mill in the Cowpe Valley, and after sixteen years without strong drink, broke pledge 'under the influence' as the *Times* put it, 'of some sore trouble'. In an effort to rescue him, 250 members of the Bethesda and Scout Bottom Blue Ribbon Club marched five abreast to his house and sang him a temperance hymn.

If the teetotallers failed to achieve the wholesale closure of the district's licensed premises, they certainly succeeded in restricting the opening of new ones. A Rawtenstall speculator, who put up a building in King Street in 1883, was refused permission to use it as a public house. He then approached the temperance crusaders, who rented it as a Blue Ribbon club.

When the excitement died down in the mid-1880s, Rossendale was left with a vigorous teetotal community, which exercised considerable influence well into the following century. Many of the Blue Ribbon clubs had a long life, and that at Helmshore, which was the last in England, survived until 1932.

Chapter 11

The Opal of the West

As well as injecting new life and ideas into the Valley, several business leaders made an impact elsewhere. In 1860, eight men from Bacup and Stacksteads formed the Rosegreave Commercial Company, which built the Royal Oak Mill in Oswaldtwistle. Others from the district chose Rishton, where Victoria Mill, like its neighbour, was known as the 'Bacup Co-op'. Another Bacup venture, the Lancashire & Yorkshire Cotton Manufacturing & Mining Company, built Spa Mill in Osset during the early 1860s.

A more lasting reminder of this enterprising spirit is the seaside town of St Anne's, which Rossendale stone and money conjured from a square mile of desolate sand hills during the final quarter of the nineteenth century.

The infant town was fortunate in capturing the interest of William John Porritt, a Helmshore woollen manufacturer, who not only built splendid houses, but also took charge of the venture at a critical moment. More than any other person he was responsible for the resort's success.

Porritt, however, was not one of the original promoters of the St Anne's-on-the-Sea Land and Building Company, which was registered in October, 1874, and which held its meetings in the Queen's Hotel, Rawtenstall. The directors, all from Bacup, Rawtenstall and Haslingden, were textile men, who were brought together by Elijah Hargreaves (1831–1904), a leading figure in the Rossendale cotton industry. At the age of seven, he began work at the Whiteheads' Lower Mill in Rawtenstall. He rose to be manager, achieving local fame by trying to save Fold Mill from being destroyed by fire and, when all was lost, leaping to safety from an upper window.

Hargreaves helped to 'float' several cotton mills during the 1860s, and by the time he visited the site of St Anne's during the summer of 1874, he had accumulated a large fortune. Walking among the sand dunes, which were crossed by only a single road and the Lytham to Blackpool railway, Hargreaves conceived the idea of a new town and at once sought out the agent for the Clifton estate, of which the coastal strip formed a part.

In Thomas Fair, he found a sympathetic listener, who had already drawn a plan for a coastal resort. Their discussions led to the formation of a public company, which took 600 acres (roughly a square mile) on a 999-year lease. This was less than Fair's scheme, but it was enough – sometimes more than enough – for the eight directors, headed by Joseph Wood Whitehead, of Alder Grange, Rawtenstall, As well as having to pay an annual ground rent of nearly £3,000, they were obliged to spend within three years some £70,000 on laying out the town and providing essential services. From the prospectus, it was clear that the board intended St Anne's to be superior to its northern neighbour:

> Of late years, Blackpool has become so much the resort of excursionists that a decided want is felt for a watering place, which, while possessing the same bracing atmosphere and commanding position on the coast as Blackpool, shall secure a more select and better class of visitors.

The architects were Maxwell and Tuke, of Bury, who had been responsible for Southport Winter Gardens and mills and other buildings in Rossendale and who were to design Blackpool Tower. One of the partners, James Maxwell, of Haslingden, was appointed the company's agent and manager.

Work on the Promenade began in February, 1875, but so uncongenial were the conditions that the labourers left in despair and replacements had to be recruited. As their wooden huts sprang up among the sand dunes, St Anne's resembled a Wild West frontier town. William Davenport built a log store and Clement Rawstron from Bacup a log cabin to which a tent was attached to provide a dining-room for the workers.

'Punctually at twelve o'clock,' Maxwell recalled, 'you might see a race for dinner, for it often happened that there were more requiring to be fed than there was food for; and to work all day in the invigorating air of St. Anne's was no small hardship'.

The number of labourers soon exceeded 200, many of whom came each day on a special train from Lytham. The foundation stone of the St Anne's Hotel was laid on 31 March by six-year-old John Talbot Clifton, grandson of the local squire. Whitehead, the company chairman, who presented the boy with a silver trowel and a polished mallet, told the guests that the venture had been successful 'beyond expectation.' A large sum of money had been subscribed and the directors intended to proceed as quickly as possible both in building and letting land to others who wished to build on their own account.

In its report of the stone-laying, the *Preston Guardian* said:

> The broad streets are to be laid out in gently curved lines, and the houses will be well back from the wide roads, from which they will be separated by large front gardens ... The centre of the town will have its 'lung' in a well laid-out pleasure ground or public park called 'The Oval'... A pier will run out 300 yards and will have at its extreme end an assembly room with orchestra.

Among the guests at the dinner which followed was William John Porritt, who would make Maxwell and Tuke's dream a reality. Angus Muir, in his unpublished *History of Porritt & Spencer* wrote:

> It was during the meal that an idea took root in his mind. Why should he not help to stimulate the growth of this seaside hamlet that looked across the Irish Sea? In many ways Porritt was a man ahead of his time, and he believed that the day would surely come – and come quickly – when people who lived in the industrial towns of Lancashire would be prepared to travel some distance daily

to get away from the environment of their works into the green countryside or to some pleasant place by the sea. A railway line from Preston ran along the coast and linked St. Anne's with many industrial towns. Not only did Porritt anticipate that there would be many applications for plots upon which seaside homes could be built, but he reckoned that retired people would look upon St. Anne's as a placid haven in which to end their days. Before he went to bed that night, he decided to put this to the test, and he proceeded to buy a considerable area of land which could be laid out in building plots.

W. J. Porritt (1828–1896) came from a family which had been in the woollen trade – first in the West Riding and then in east Lancashire – for more than 200 years. At their mills in Edenfield, Stubbins and Bamford, his father and two uncles pioneered the manufacture of industrial fabrics, in particular the felts which covered the drying cylinders of the newly-invented paper-making machines. Porritt moved to Helmshore with his father and two brothers in 1866, when trouble over river pollution restricted their activities at Edenfield. They bought the Midgehole and Sunnybank estates and within two years had completed a substantial four-storey mill, which, like the nearby workers' houses and Porritt's own mansion at Torside, was built from stone quarried in Alden. A correspondent of *The Paper Trade Journal* of America wrote in 1879 that of the many factories he had visited in various parts of the world, Sunnybank was the finest 'for arrangement, machinery and solidity of premises'.

The mill's success was based on the excellence of its products. 'I want something better than the best,' was one of Porritt's sayings; and with his thorough knowledge of the trade, he knew at a glance when goods fell short of perfection.

Orders grew in line with demand for machine-made paper, which was stimulated by a number of factors, including the abolition of the stamp duty on newspapers in 1855, the introduction of compulsory education in 1870 and the much greater use of paper and cardboard by the retail trades. The UK production of machine-made paper rose from 100,000 tons a year in the early 1860s to more than 250,000 tons at the end of the '70s. Lancashire became one of the country's leading paper-making centres, its mills almost doubling their output between 1865 and 1875. Helmshore supplied its felts to Germany, the United States and other countries; and though Sunnybank's profit were large, they were regularly invested in the business. Porritt, during the 1860s, paid himself only £5 10s. a fortnight; and when his two sons went into the mill as teenagers, they received the standard wage of 2s. a week. Though Porritt spent large sums on expansion – he acquired Higher Mill in 1880 – and on extending his estates, he had money to spare for developing St Anne's.

Having bought his building land, Porritt waited for the applications to flow in, but in the words of Augustus Muir:

> He was both surprised and disappointed that his plots on one of the most delightful parts of the Lancashire coastline did not seem to appeal to anyone. He did his best to conceal his chagrin. He was convinced that St. Annes did have a great future. 'If people do not have the imagination to realize how pleasant it would be to live there', he said, 'I shall show them by building the houses myself'. This meant expenditure of much more money than he had expected to sink into the venture. Then he came to another decision. He would erect substantial houses of the beautiful sandstone from the quarries of his Helmshore estates. One after another the houses were erected, and made a fine array on the green slopes above the shore road from Lytham to Blackpool ... Before very long Porritt found that his St. Anne's-on-the-Sea speculation was costing him sums of money that ran into six figures. Was it time, he wondered, to pull in his hands?

The early burst of activity, during which the price of the company's shares rose by 50 per cent, was followed by stagnation. 'Men fought shy of the scheme and decided to lock up their money for their grandchildren,' said Maxwell. The company several times changed its bankers to secure larger overdrafts; Maxwell resigned after a row with the board; the shares fell to well below their issue price; shareholders demanded inquiries; the directors halved their fees, but bankruptcy grew ever closer. The company had even to threaten Elijah Hargreaves with court action for non-payment of his ground rent.

It was now that Porritt took decisive control of the faltering development. A large part of his fortune had been sunk in the new town and he seriously considered whether or not he should get out before all was lost. Augustus Muir wrote of these difficult days:

> Porritt was a man with very steady nerves, and if there was anything he disliked it was being beaten. A writer in a local paper said that, at the time when the project was at its lowest ebb, 'Mr Porritt was perhaps the only one who had faith in its ultimate success'. In recalling his thoughts at that time, he said that he examined the profits that were being earned at Sunnybank, and this gave him courage to go forward. More and more of those windows of the elegant Porritt houses had curtains in them; more and more of those chimneys were smoking. Good news spreads, and a short time after he had decided to back his venture up to the hilt he felt he was on the way to success. He had sunk upwards of a quarter of a million sterling to carry out his ideals, and as he was the largest shareholder in the place, folk began to call him 'the Father of St. Anne's.' and asked him to take various public offices … As he looked back on his early days on the coast and talked about his heavy commitments there, he would give a humorous shrug and say that it would have all but ruined him if his courage had failed him at the critical point.

Porritt became chairman of the company in April, 1881, and remained in office until his death, but as late as 1892, he was writing to an American business friend, who had asked him for financial backing, 'My available funds have been seriously straitened … The drain which St. Anne's now makes upon me is very heavy still, and it has to be constantly met for the progress of the place'.

Though the worries of creating a new town were great, Porritt did not miss an opportunity for a celebration when it was justified. To mark the opening of the pier on 15 June 1885, he closed his mills, hired a train, engaged the village brass band and took his workpeople to the new town. There had been suggestions that few would attend the ceremony, but the fears were groundless. Blackpool and Lytham as well as Helmshore sent their contingents.

The Land and Building Company was frequently accused of giving the pier higher priority than sewers; and it was not until 1892 that the critics were silenced. On 18 August Porritt cut the first sod of the sewage works and used the occasion to entertain his 600 Helmshore employees once more. 'A more munificent holiday was never given by a master to his workpeople,' said the *Haslingden Guardian*. By now the population of St Anne's was almost 4,000; moreover, added the *Guardian*, 'the number of first-class railway passenger contracts to and from the town is larger than from Blackpool'.

The success of St Anne's was assured, and in the final years of his life Porritt began to reap the benefits of his perseverance and enterprise. He died on 30 October 1896. Elijah Hargreaves lived until 1906, having returned to the board of the Land and Building Company and having interested himself in several undertakings in Blackpool. He became a director of the Central Pier Company, but preferred to live in St Anne's.

Chapter 12

A Bacup 'adventure'

'When I was at Bacup I felt that I was living through a page of puritan history.' Now that's a quotation to raise a few eyebrows, even in Bacup itself. Yet it was written in all seriousness by a famous Englishwoman whose visits to the town in the 1880s had far-reaching consequences.

Beatrice Potter, later Mrs Sidney Webb, was twenty five when she had the 'daring' idea of visiting her relatives in Rossendale. It was adventurous because it meant crossing the 'class barrier', a thing almost unknown for a well-bred Victorian lady. Miss Potter's links with Bacup were through her maternal grandparents. Her grandfather, Lawrence Heyworth, a successful woollen manufacturer, who became a rich Liverpool merchant and a Member of Parliament, chose for his wife a cousin who worked in a Bacup mill. It was to visit the working-class members of her grandmother's family that Miss Potter set out in 1883. The go-between was her old nurse, a relative of these cousins; and she arranged for Beatrice, in the guise of 'Miss Jones', a Welsh farmer's daughter to accompany her from the Potter mansion on the Welsh border to the humble cottage of John Ashworth, chapel keeper, in Irwell Terrace.

'On a wet November evening,' wrote the future social reformer, 'we picked our way along the irregularly-paved and badly-lighted back streets of Bacup to the old-fashioned house at the back of the chapel. We were received by a regular old puritan and his daughter in the most hearty fashion, prayers being offered up for our safety and spiritual wellbeing while under their roof.'

The whole area, she noted, seemed deserted and 'there was that curious stillness in the air which overtakes a manufacturing town when the mills with their noise and their lights are closed and the mill hands are "cleaning up" or enjoying "biffin" by their own fireside'.

'Miss Jones' discovered that three things dominated the lives of most townspeople – the mill, the chapel and the co-operative store. She studied all of them as part of 'my first attempt to investigate conditions of labour'.

Factory legislation was indispensable, she quickly decided. 'My cousins would return home late in the evening quite worn out with the day's toil. I felt grieved to see the way in which their interest in other things had to be subordinated to the long and ceaseless grind of work.'

But despite their hard lives, the mill workers displayed 'a simple piety' which impressed the visitor. 'One thing which struck me greatly was the moral refinement of these humble folk. They talked in such a quaint, beautiful manner that it seemed like a page of *Pilgrim's Progress*. Their language was quite classical. These were chapel people taking part in the various organizations of the religious community to which they belonged, and I realized what a splendid training ground the chapel is for social self-government.

Beatrice Potter was in Bacup from 7 November to the 20th. On the final Sunday, she visited a local chapel,

> where I heard a grand sermon from a Dissenting minister, without culture, who had been a farmer the first part of his life and had left his work only when called upon by the divine spirit ... I was strongly moved as I listened to the words of that thin, spare-looking man, whose whole frame seemed shaken by the earnestness of his spirit; and in silence I renewed the vow that I would work for the cause of goodness and truth; and prayed that I may be shown the way clearly.

Religion was a subject to which Miss Potter returned when she visited Bacup again in October, 1886, staying with other relatives at 5 Angel Street in Tong Lane. She disclosed her identity at the end of her visit; and in a letter to her father, she wrote, 'This is the only society I have ever lived in, in which religious faith really guides thought and action, and forms the basis of the whole life of the community.'

Through a cousin, who worked in a co-operative store, Beatrice Potter first became interested in the movement which, in Rossendale, embraced not only shop keeping, but also the running of cotton mills. 'Class spirit hardly exists. There is no bitter, uneasy feeling among the inhabitants of Bacup, for there is practically social equality,' she noted. And because so many working people had shares in co-operative mills, 'there is a recognised desire to keep down wages'.

In her diary she wrote, 'Public opinion, which means religiously-guided opinion, presses heavily on the mis-doer or non-worker. There are no attractions for those who have not sources of love and interest within them: no work for those who cannot or will not work constantly.'

Today, it takes an effort to think of Bacup as a proletarian utopia. Things have changed, as Beatrice Potter feared they would. 'One wonders,' she wrote in 1886, 'what will happen when the religious feeling of the people is undermined by advancing scientific culture?' The well-filled chapels have gone, that in Irwell Terrace among them. Angel Street has been demolished, so that Bacup no longer has a tangible link with the woman who, by her advocacy of collectivism, did so much to change our way of life. But as Beatrice Potter herself wrote, 'The Bacup adventure gave me a decisive turn to my self-development. It was there I decided to become an investigator of social institutions.'

Chapter 13

THE FIRST IQ TEST

IS IT A GOOD IDEA to make a pie crust ornamental rather than plain? The question is of historical importance since it was included in the world's first public IQ test, held in Haslingden on 13 December 1903. To learn how the town gained this distinction we must go back to 1900, when Mr (later Sir) William Mather, a Manchester industrialist and the MP for Rossendale, presented prizes to students who attended classes arranged by the Haslingden Technical Instruction Committee. During his speech, Mather said he would like to give a prize for intelligence, which he defined as the ability to use knowledge, the yardstick being how quickly and how far we apply in ordinary life what we have mentally stored up.

Deeply worried by the way British firms were being outperformed by their German competitors, Mather wondered whether or not our rivals were working harder or applying their intelligence more profitably. Suitable tests might help the British to catch up.

On the platform that evening was Henry Holman (1859–1919), an Inspector of Schools who was known through his books and articles as 'an educational idealist'. Mather's suggestion took his fancy and he set out to devise an examination which would test intelligence rather than the ability to memorise facts.

This brings us back to the pie crust, the ornamentation or otherwise of which exercised the minds of seventy four young men and women on that December evening in 1903. The answers have not survived, but Holman supplied his own once he had marked the papers. Yes, he said, there is a point in taking pains over pie crusts, for 'that which pleases the eye tempts the appetite. A pleasant frame of mind tends to organic brightness and, therefore, good digestion.'

Not all of Holman's questions were as straightforward as that. Many were thought freakish, but the test, nevertheless, aroused countrywide interest. 'The effect of Mr Holman's paper,' reported the *Haslingden Gazette*, 'has been to develop such a mania for catchy conundrums that life in the town has scarcely been bearable this last week. When you have met a friend, the first thing that he has done has been to try you with the "intelligence" question as to your choice of a ton of sovereigns of two tons of half sovereigns, which question, by the way, is more sure to trip one when it is spoken than when it is on paper. Hundreds of people in Haslingden have been floored by that question'.

The writer believed that Holman had undertaken a task that 'was beyond accomplishment'. Nevertheless, a young weaver in a local cotton mill, John Thomas Heap, scored high marks and won Mather's £5 prize.

It was some years before the intelligence tests we know today became a familiar feature of our lives. The symbols with their hidden patterns may do the job better than 'Mr Holman's Christmas Crackers', as the *Gazette* dubbed the questions, but one might be forgiven for believing that an occasional inquiry about ornamental pie crusts would make the modern tests more appetising.

Chapter 14

ELECTRIC SHOCKS

From a short sentence, appended almost as an afterthought to the report of a lantern lecture, readers of the *Bacup and Rossendale News* learned in March, 1864, that one of the century's most important scientific discoveries had been seen in Rawtenstall. 'The lecturer also exhibited the electric light,' the account concluded, leaving everyone to wonder what the audience in the Haslingden Road School thought of Mr P. O. Whitehead's demonstration and why, indeed, he came to give it.

Though a number of impressive displays had been staged in Lancashire, electric light remained little more than a curiosity. The arc lamps then available burned out too quickly to make them attractive, and Rossendale saw no more of the new light until March, 1878, when William Brooks, later the 2nd Baron Crawshaw, gave a lecture (of which more later) in Crawshawbooth. The *Bacup Times* said that a lamp, which he ran from a battery, produced a 'very fine effect', though less of a sensation than other electrical wonders.

> On the platform was a splendid man-of-war with men and guns mounted. This was floating in water with a torpedo under it, and was connected by 18 wires to the lecturer's table. A battery fort was also erected with men and 16 guns mounted. The whole of these were fired by means of high-tension fuses merely by the lecturer pressing a button in his hand. An induction coil could give a one-inch spark and the ship was blown up and sunk by the torpedo, to the immense delight of the audience.

In November, 1878, electric lights shone brightly at Haslingden, when the town's football club promoted two floodlit matches in conjunction with a Manchester company, which had invested heavily in arc lamps and portable generators. Both games – one under Association rules against Edgworth, the other Rugby Union against Bacup – attracted more than 8,000 spectators, the 'gate' money exceeding £100 on each occasion. The four lamps on the Rye Hill ground were 'very brilliant' and gave 'great satisfaction'. These games were among the very first to be played under lights, but despite immense public interest, the novelty had only a short life. Rather less successful than the football matches was a display by the Manchester company in the Co-operative Hall, Rawtenstall, a few days later. Advertisements promised that a musical entertainment in aid of Kay Street Baptist Chapel would be illuminated by two lamps with a combined strength of 12,000 candles. This may have been so for part of the concert, but there were periods, said the *Times*, when the lights grew 'very dim' and 'twice both went out, which caused a laugh and stopped Miss Smith in her singing'. The *Times* described the attendance as moderate, but the *News* said about 800 people, including some of the gentry of the district, went to see 'this wonderful discovery'.

The year 1878 also saw the discovery by both Joseph Swan and Thomas Edison of the longer-lasting incandescent lamp. Permanent installations soon followed and it looked at the start of 1880 as though Haslingden would be the first town in the country to have an electrically-lighted mill. According to the *Bacup Times* of 17 January:

> The directors of one of the largest manufacturing companies in Haslingden have made arrangements with the Edison Electric Light Company to introduce the electric light into their works; and the agents are so confident of success that they have offered to forfeit all remuneration in case of failure to light up the works at the present price of Haslingden gas.

The scheme did not go forward and no more was heard of industrial lighting until November, 1883, when Sir J. C. Lee and Company replaced 450 gas lamps at Loveclough Print Works with 260 electric lights of

20 candle power each. The *Times* considered the new system a great improvement on the old. Bacup saw the light in 1884, when the corn mill of William Sutcliffe & Son, near the town centre, switched on 26 of Swan's lamps. They gave great satisfaction, and when, two years later, the firm built a new mill next to Rawtenstall railway station, electricity was preferred to gas, prompting the *News* to praise the 'brilliant effect'.

In spite of these ventures, the new system was adopted slowly, the great disadvantage in Rossendale being the lack of a central generating station. Though the gas companies remained complacent, there was no doubting that electricity provided a far superior light. This point was made by a *Times* reporter who visited an exhibition staged by the Bacup Natural History Society at the Mechanics' Institution in 1889. 'The brilliance and steadiness of the light, he wrote, 'was very conspicuous compared with the jaundiced appearance of the gas light'.

In 1892, the Queen's Hotel in Rawtenstall became the first in Rossendale to install electric lights. Two years later, Mr G. A. Smith, of Flaxmoss House, Helmshore, joined the converts, to be followed in November of the same year by the members of Bacup Liberal Club and the directors of Holden and Company, the Bacup tea and general dealers. Six lamps of 50 candle power lit the lecture room and six others with half that power illuminated the billiard table. The opening of the tea dealers' new premises created 'an extraordinary amount of public interest', the main attraction being the electric light, which, as the *Times* noted, 'is now adopted for the first time in Bacup for shop illuminating purposes'. The Haslingden Co-operative Society and Flash Mills, Haslingden, were other early users of electric light, though both were outshone by W. H. Trickett ('The Slipper King'), whose arcade in Waterfoot – opened in March, 1899 – had four and a half miles of wire, 500 lamps and an 'engine room' to provide the power. 'The lights in each room can be turned on and off at pleasure,' said the *Times* reporter, much impressed with his first encounter with a switch.

Street lighting began in the late 1890s, thanks to the Haslingden, Rawtenstall and Bacup Outfall Sewerage Board, which, for ten years provided free electricity for twenty five lamps between Ewood Bridge and Irwell Vale.

Chapter 15

'The Wonderful Telephone'

'The telegraph is at last superseded by the Wonderful Telephone,' declared a London novelties company in 1878, when, for five shillings and nine pence, it offered readers of the *Bacup Times* the components of a simple working model.

The Londoners were clearly unaware that Rossendale already had the 'wonder', an account of which appeared in the same edition of the same issue of the newspaper. It was no toy, but a system which could link buildings on opposite sides of a street. William Brooks we have already met, and 'this gentleman and scholar' as well as showing electric light, demonstrated his telephone to members of the Crawshawbooth Literary and Mechanics' Institution on 7 March during a lecture in the Co-operative Hall.

> The telephone wires were carried to the Wesleyan School, a distance of nearly 200 yards, when solos on the cornet and songs rendered in the school were clearly and distinctly heard by the audience in the hall; a conversation was also carried on between the two places.

The *Times* reported the event matter-of-factly under the headline 'Lecture by W Brooks Esq., BA,' failing to realise that what had taken place in the village was one of the first successful public demonstrations in Britain. The device, which had been patented as recently as 1876, had yet to be exploited commercially; and it was

18 days after the Crawshawbooth experiment that the inventor, Alexander Graham Bell, predicted that telephones would one day connect houses, shops and factories and eventually different cities.

William Brooks came from a family with interests in calico printing at Sunnyside, quarrying, coal mining and property development. He was educated at Rugby and Oxford, where he learned about electricity which became his hobby. When he claimed a vote as occupier of Sunnyside House in 1879 – he was then 26 – the *Bacup and Rossendale News* noted that 'there is a telephone in one room and other rooms contain instruments used by Mr Brooks in his scientific pursuits'.

Though Brooks may well have provided the Sunnyside works with a telephone, the earliest recorded installation in Rossendale was in 1881, when J. S. Sutcliffe connected his home, Beech House in Todmorden Road, Bacup, to his corn mill 400 yards away. Five years later, the first link with other districts was provided by the Lancashire and Cheshire Telephone Exchange Company. The *Times* of June 16 reported:

> Telephonic communication has been established between Irwell Springs Dye Works (Messrs Steiner & Co.) and the Church works of the same company. A special wire has been erected by way of Nooking End, Deerplay, Burnley Wood and Holmes Chapel. There is also a communication with Dunkenhalgh House (the residence of Mr Kerr) and the Manchester Office, 34 York Street. The first message was transmitted yesterday week [28 May] and was entirely successful. Since then there has been daily communication between the places mentioned.

The *News*, which published a similar account, commented, 'The telephone has been used for some time in the district in a small way, but no part has previously been connected with the large area taken in by the telephone company.'

'Haslingden and Rawtenstall are now united by telephone,' the *Rossendale Free Press* announced in October, 1886, in praising the enterprise of Messrs Sudall and Furness, a firm of clothiers with a shop in each town.

> Their constantly-growing business has assumed such proportions that inter-communication between the two establishments was of hourly occurrence, and having carefully calculated the sums spent in telegrams, 'bus letters and conveyances, they concluded that the cheapest and most effective substitute was the telephone … We had the opportunity of speaking through it, and the ease and distinctness with which the slightest intonation of the voice is discernible, proves beyond doubt its great ability.

In December, 1886, Thomas Williams, an electrical engineer, who lived in Baxenden, installed 'Sylvanus P. Thompson's patent telephone' at the Haslingden Commercial Company's three cotton mills (Paghouse, Holden Vale and Old Carr New Shed) and later used a letter from the company to support his advertisements in the local press.

> The telephones you fixed for us between our three mills some two months ago are working satisfactorily. At one of the mills the instrument is in a room where the noise is very great, but we have found this to be no deterrent, the words coming from the office being heard as distinctly as in the other instruments.

The Bacup Carriage Company, which ran horse buses through the Valley and to Rochdale and Burnley, linked its office in Pippin Bank to the George and Dragon Hotel, the Bacup terminus and to the King Street stables in 1887.

Useful though these installations were, they had a limited value, and urgent messages to and from distant parts of the country had to go by telegraph, a method vigorously encouraged by the railway companies. Rossendale saw its first telegraph poles during the summer of 1852, when the Magnetic Telegraph Company's engineers advanced from Manchester along the lines of the East Lancashire Railway.

In September, the *Blackburn Standard* reported that men were busily attaching the wires, which were soon to serve both the railway company and the public. All Rossendale telegrams were sent and received at railway stations until 1866, when the British and Irish Magnetic Telegraph Company opened an office in the Bacup Mechanics' Institution. The *Times* congratulated the company on its prompt delivery service and said in May, 1867, that business was 'considerable because of it'.

The Post Office, which was granted a monopoly of inland telegraph business in 1869, found an unusual customer, for as the *News* reported on 7 July, 1877:

> All Bacupians, who have been put to inconvenience by the general inaccuracy of clocks [in the town] – and there are very few who have not – will be pleased to hear that we are now going to have exact Greenwich time every morning at 10 o'clock. Mr D. Hargreaves, watchmaker, of Market Street, having contracted with the Government for the supply thereof by means of electricity. At considerable cost, Mr Hargreaves has procured from the London makers an electric contrivance which stands in his shop, to communicate with which a wire has been laid to meet the wires at the Bacup Post Office; and every morning at exactly 10 o'clock, for a few minutes before and after which hour all telegraphic messages are suspended throughout the United Kingdom, an electric current passes from the Greenwich Observatory, giving the time all over the country. A large ball, called a time ball, surmounts the contrivance and when the current comes into contact with the works, the ball immediately drops, thus indicating the correct Greenwich time.

Though the telephone was held in law to be a form of telegraph, the Post Office left its early development to private enterprise. And enterprising the pioneers sometimes were, providing the *Times* of 4 October 1890, with the most arresting headline it ever printed: 'An Opera Performed in Manchester Heard in Bacup'.

> Last evening [said the report] an interesting telephone experiment was tried in Bacup at the new exchange of the National Telephone Co. in Market Street. The Prince's Theatre in Manchester, where Carl Rosa's Opera Company was performing *La Traviata*, was connected by telephone to the Bacup Exchange, and we were invited to hear the result, which proved a great treat. The various songs, duets and choruses were heard quite distinctly and it was easy to recognise the voices of the principal vocalists. The orchestral accompaniments, the crescendos and diminuendos and the applause following each performance were also easily noticeable.

The exchange opened on 8 October, with private subscribers paying £9 a year and businesses £12. Non-subscribers paid sixpence for each call. The company also opened exchanges at 29 Deardengate, Haslingden, and 2 Barlow Street, Rawtenstall.

The success of the operatic eavesdropping contrasted strongly with the telegraphic disaster, which occurred only two months later when Rossendale received its first visit from a British prime minister. Newspapers in those days printed everything leading politicians had to say and they sent to public meetings teams of reporters who took down and transcribed the speeches, which were handed in short 'takes' to the telegraph staff for transmission.

Lord Salisbury opened Waterfoot Conservative Club on 3 December 1890, and spoke on the same evening to 6,500 people (reserved platform seats cost a guinea each) in the new Myrtle Grove Mill. In the previous week, the *Rossendale Division Gazette* reported that 80 reporters were expected to cover the meeting, adding that

> A room has been specially fitted up for the telegraph clerks and several rows of substantial benches have been erected so that the telegraphic instruments can be securely fixed. When the operators are all at work the scene will be one of the most remarkable ever seen in Rossendale and will afford striking evidence of the science of telegraphy for, if the weather is favourable, the transmitters will, it is expected, be able to send 350 words a minute.

These elaborate arrangements were largely in vain, not because of the weather, but because the wires were badly insulated. Few words reached their destinations and, as the *Times* noted, 'Many of the morning papers were unable to publish a report of Lord Salisbury's speech, while others received only part of it.

By 1900, The National Telephone Company had installed 160 telephones between Bacup and Rising Bridge – No. 1 was at Oak House, the home of J. Craven Hoyle – but there was at least one Rossendalian who wanted something better. He described his endeavours to a *Times* reporter in August, 1905.

> I had the opportunity of witnessing a demonstration of wireless telegraphy. It will doubtless come as a surprise to readers to hear that this took place in Bacup, and still more will it surprise them to hear that before long a new system is likely to be practical operation between Bacup and Waterfoot. Such, however, is likely to be the case, Dr Brown, of Burwood House having obtained a licence for the installation of the Marconi system of wireless telegraphy between his residence in Todmorden Road, Bacup, and his surgery in Waterfoot. Mr Robert Brown, the youngest son of Dr Brown, who for some time has been studying the science of electricity, has to a considerable extent been responsible for the construction of the apparatus and he it was who gave the practical demonstration in the Mechanics' Institution. The despatching apparatus stood on a table in the news room and the receiving apparatus was on another table in the old schoolroom. There was, of course, absolutely no connection except by the natural elements of earth and air, but they were sufficient for Mr Brown to send through for my edification some short messages and to show that his ability to set up apparatus has been equal to the task. It is interesting to note that since the Wireless Telegraphy Act came into operation last year, only 18 applications for licences have been granted and one of these has come to Bacup.

Chapter 16

FLYING BOILERS

It is surprising how far a large mill boiler will fly if the pressure inside becomes too great for the strained metal to withstand. On such occasions, steam power gains an awesome new dimension, propelling the boiler like a rocket with catastrophic and spectacular results. Rossendale witnessed two such disasters during the nineteenth century.

On the morning of 9 June 1858, a boiler at Spring Mill, Dean, leapt from its bed and was blown in two, the sections going in opposite directions at enormous speed. One section demolished a warehouse, scattering stones over a wide area, and then separated. The larger piece fell eighteen yards from the mill; the smaller travelled six yards more before landing on a wall. The other section of the boiler, said *The Illustrated London News*,

> forced its way through a breast wall a yard in thickness and cut a trench two yards deep through a cart track, displacing about twelve tons of earth. It knocked down the wall between the high road and an adjoining field, and finally rested in the field, thirty yards from the road, having altogether traversed a distance of forty-eight yards through all the obstacles named.

The blast from the explosion blew down the blacksmith's shop and most of the weaving shed. It also 'caused another boiler to be torn up and reared almost on one end'.

The alarmed workpeople [the report continues] were rushing frantically from the place when a flue, which conveys steam from the boiler to the opposite end of the mill, burst, and thirteen or fourteen workpeople were enveloped in and scalded by the steam. Hannah Howarth was so severely scalded that she expired the same day. Thomas Nuttall was seen working at a hooking machine a few minutes before the explosion. He was afterwards found where he had been hurled across the warehouse, about ten yards distant, and quite dead. Hargreaves Lord was crossing the warehouse when he was struck down by the falling building; and when found, he was lying under a large stone and quite dead. Fifteen other persons were injured, some of them seriously.

The second disaster occurred at Hutch Bank Mill, Haslingden, on 15 October, 1875, the boiler rising through two floors of the building before emerging from the roof into the open air. It continued its ascent, grazed the mill chimney and carried off the lightning conductor. The *Bacup Times* estimated that the boiler – twenty four feet long and seven feet in diameter – reached a height of seventeen yards, after which it 'alighted on one end and rolled over as if it had been a thing of life'. The boiler came down seventy yards from the mill and only five from a dye-house. 'Notwithstanding its aerial flight, and the obstructions it encountered,' commented the newspaper, 'it does not appear to have sustained any damage and so far as can be seen, none of its parts are missing'.

Stones from the disintegrating mill were flung in all directions and several were found embedded in the ground two hundred yards away. Only one life was lost: a boy named Walton was taken from the wreckage, but died soon afterwards. Crowds of people left their work and hurried to the scene; and on the following Saturday and Sunday thousands of sightseers travelled to Haslingden in special trains from as far off as Manchester.

Chapter 17

A NOVEL ENCOUNTER

In which English novel does the hero propose marriage, successfully as it turns out, while sitting under a dry-stone wall on the moors above Bacup? Few Rossendalians or, indeed, students of English literature, could give a ready answer, yet the novel was well read in its day and went through several editions. *The History of David Grieve*, by Mrs Humphrey Ward, was published in 1892, and like most of the author's works, it has strong religious overtones. Today, its interest lies in its descriptive passages, of which the following is a good example.

> At last, after a steep and muddy climb through uninviting back ways, they were out on the moor. An apology for a moor in David's eyes! For the hills which surround the valley of the Irwell are, for the most part, green and rolling ground, heatherless and cragless. Still, from the top they looked over a wide and wind-blown scene, the bolder moors of Rochdale behind them, and in front the long green basin in which the Irwell rises. Along the valley bottoms lay the mills, with their surrounding rows of small stone houses. Up on the backs of the moors crouched the old farms, which have watched the mills come and will perhaps see them go; and here and there a grim-looking colliery marked a fold of the hill. The landscape on a spring day has a bracing bareness, which is not without exhilaration. The wind blows freely, the sun lies broadly on the hills. England, on the whole at her busiest and best spreads before you.

In another passage about Bacup, Mrs Ward writes:

> All the people worked in two large spinning mills, or in a few smaller factories representing dependent industries, such as reed making ... Socially everybody knew everybody. They were passionately interested in each other's lives. And their religion, of a strong Protestant type, expressed in various forms of dissent, formed an ideal bond which kept the little society together and made an authority which all acknowledged and in which all moved.

Mrs Ward was writing of Bacup, from where she had walked to the source of the Irwell. There, 'under one of the mortarless stone walls which streak the moors', she set the scene of the proposal.

> Pigeons passed overhead, going and coming from an old farm about a hundred yards away; the sky above them had a lark for voice, singing his loudest; and in the next field a peewit was wheeling and crying. The few trees in sight were struggling fast into leaf. Nature even in this cold north was gay today and young.

What, you will be wondering, was Mrs Ward, grand-daughter of Dr Arnold of Rugby and niece of Matthew Arnold, the poet, doing in Bacup? The visit was arranged by Beatrice Webb, the Socialist pioneer, whose grandfather, a wealthy local manufacturer, had married a pretty mill girl. Mrs Webb sought out her working-class relations and stayed with them on several occasions. When Mrs Ward needed mill town material for her novel, the outcome was a visit to Rossendale.

Mrs Ward's novels are little read nowadays and it is hard to believe that her best-seller, *Robert Elsmere*, which attacked evangelical Christianity, sold 70,000 copies, in this country and more than half a million in the States. Gladstone replied to it, and the novel and his response were at one time given away with bars of soap. For *David Grieve*, which came next, Macmillan paid £7,000, making the bits about Bacup the most expensive fiction ever written on a Lancashire subject.

Chapter 18

RUNAWAY TRAINS

THE NOVELTY AND EXCITEMENT of travelling by train in the early days of steam owed much to the unpredictable behaviour of the rolling stock. Runaway trains whizzed through Ramsbottom on several occasions, and twice at least there were multiple mishaps of the kind one sees in slapstick films. The first occurred on 28 December 1857, when wagons laden with stone broke away from a train in Grane Road sidings – between Helmshore and Haslingden – and ran down the line towards Stubbins Junction three miles away. The guard, who had neglected to place pieces of timber between the spokes, jumped aboard the retreating wagons, but fell off near Helmshore station. Catch points were not then in use, nor could anything be done to warn the driver of an approaching passenger train. So violent was the collision that the last two carriages were uncoupled and began to move backwards. In one compartment were Henry Hargreaves and his sister, both from Blackburn, and in another a Mr Littlewood.

Both men opened a door, and, as the *Blackburn Standard* put it, 'Mr Hargreaves asked Mr Littlewood's opinion as to what was best to be done in the hope of effecting their escape'. Mr shouted back that leaping out was their only hope. With the carriages rapidly gaining speed, Mr Hargreaves took this advice and landed on the embankment, knocking himself out, but breaking no bones. Seeing her brother lying motionless by the track, Miss Hargreaves felt unable to follow. Mr Littlewood also hesitated and it was not until the carriages had shot through Ramsbottom that he flung himself out and was seriously hurt. Miss Hargreaves, in the words of the *Bury Times*, 'was hurried on through tunnels and over bridges until the impetus was exhausted, which was not before the carriages had nearly reached Bury'.

The station master at Ramsbottom, 'who had seen the rapid transit of the carriages forthwith pursued them with a pilot engine and found Miss Hargreaves pacing backwards and forwards on the line near to a sawmill. He accommodated her with a seat on the tender and provided her with a covering as a protection from the rain, which was then copiously descending. Being thus made safe, she was conveyed on the tender back to Ramsbottom, where she found her brother anxiously awaiting her.'

Some eleven years later, on 19 December 1868, four wagons and the brake van of an early-morning coal train ran away at Bacup. The engine driver gave chase, but could not catch up with them. Travelling at 'a fearful rate,' they crashed into a goods train standing in Rawtenstall Station. The driver and stoker jumped clear only seconds before the collision. The brake van and one of the wagons were 'shivered into fragments,' but, as the local paper observed, 'this was not the whole extent of the disaster'. The force of the impact reversed the engine and turned the steam on at full, and the engine with two wagons set off for Ramsbottom, 'through which it passed with the speed of thought'.

The station staff at Ramsbottom, who always seemed to have a locomotive standing by, set off in pursuit. The morning was still dark and they failed to see that their quarry had run out of steam between Summerseat and Bury. The outcome was yet another crash, which blocked the line for several hours.

Chapter 19

AERIAL ADVENTURES

WHEN DID THE DUKE OF EDINBURGH take to the air in Rawtenstall? The answer: On Saturday, 23 August, 1883, the 'Duke' being a large balloon and the occasion a gala to mark the opening of the town's new temperance club. The balloon's flight to Shawforth was one of several outcomes of the immensely successful anti-drink campaign conducted throughout Rossendale by the Blue Ribbon Army.

Though passenger-carrying balloons were not unknown in Rossendale, half a century had passed since most local people had seen one. In May, 1824, Windham William Sadler, one of our first intrepid aeronauts, landed near Bacup after a short flight to mark the opening of Rochdale Gas Works, where the balloon was inflated. He and his passenger, a Mr Plath from Liverpool, heard a cuckoo and the voices of villagers 'whose noise fell on our ears like the howling of a distant pack of hounds'. On landing,

> The inhabitants of that populous neighbourhood, to whom the sight was perfectly novel, crowded around in such large numbers and with such intense curiosity that some trifling damage was done to the balloon.

In June, 1828, George Green, another famous pioneer, flew from Bury to Edenfield, dropping a kitten by parachute on the way.

For the Rawtenstall gala, held in a field opposite the church of St James the Less, the temperance campaigners engaged Captain Whelan, an aeronaut from Huddersfield, and arranged for the local gas company to lay pipes to the point of ascent. The captain, said the *Bacup Times*, 'was successful in filling the monstrous orb by about four o'clock from which time until six o'clock it rode at anchor amidst the gaze of thousands of spectators'. When inflated with 25,000 cubic feet of gas, the balloon towered seventy feet above the expectant crowd.

> At ten minutes to six, Captain Whelan stepped into the car along the Mr Jonathan Nuttall, of Wood Top, who had volunteered to accompany the aeronaut on his heavenward flight. At nine minutes to six, Captain Whelan ordered his men, who had been holding down the balloon, to let go, and up she went for a distance of about 30 feet, in which position she was held by means of a rope. After a few minutes' delay, Captain Whelan cut asunder the rope with his pen-knife, and amidst the waving of hats and handkerchiefs and the deafening shouts of the assembled multitude, the balloon proceeded upon its upward journey without the slightest hitch.

Nuttall, a working man selected at random from the crowd, was given the task of throwing out sand to control the balloon's height, and on his return to the Blue Ribbon Club in King Street, he found himself 'lionised all night' as the members called on him over and over to repeat the details of his adventure.

> After leaving the ground, I happened to look back and was surprised to see that all the people looked like one black mass. We could hear them shouting for a considerable length of time. We got into a current of air which carried us right over Rawtenstall. Another current took us in the direction of Cloughfold and Whinberry Naze, on the summit of which several children were playing, on to whom we threw a little sand, which caused them to look up and wave their handkerchiefs. We then went in the direction of Newchurch, over which we came to a standstill for about fifteen seconds. As we passed over the dog kennels at

Newchurch, the hounds set up a tremendous yell on seeing us, and the crows, on catching a glimpse of us, dropped down as if they were shot, while the horses and cattle cocked up their tails and ran about as if they were mad. They couldn't understand us, and their capers were enough to make a parson laugh.

At Bacup, the balloon reached a height of 3,025 feet. It then crossed over Stacksteads and Bacup Cemetery before coming down, 'to the great surprise of the natives', in a newly-mown meadow near the Tam o' Shanter public house in Shawforth. The grappling iron, said Nuttall, 'stuck to the ground first time. The balloon rebounded once and fell over on its sides helpless as a child. With the help of a few villagers, we put the balloon in its case and lifting it on a cart, proceeded to Shawforth station in time to catch the 6.55 pm train to Bacup.'

Chapter 20

WHEELS OF MISFORTUNE

WHAT HAS BECOME OF MANIAS? They have gone so completely out of fashion that whole generations have been denied the chance of seeing one or, indeed, of being swept along by the excitement. Nineteenth-century Rossendale produced a good crop of manias, some of which, like the Blue Ribbon temperance movement, involved huge sections of the population; others attracted smaller groups, but were no less intense. During 1869, local people were caught up in the velocipede mania and began buying, building, riding and falling off machines ranging from chainless 'Boneshakers' with two wheels to gigantic contraptions with three or four.

Among the first to leap into the saddle was a Bacup musician, who bought a two-wheeler in Liverpool with the aim of cutting the time spent on his weekly trip to Todmorden, which he had previously made on foot. 'On the level road, he seemed to get along easily enough,' said the *Bacup Times* of 17 April, 'but he had some difficulty in ascending the hill'. Soon, however, he was on a downward course and 'the velocipede appeared a great success, requiring little or no exertion'. This unfortunately was a brakeless era and 'the road becoming steeper, the velocipede gradually, but surely increased its speed and began to bound over the loose stones with anything but a comfortable jolt'.

The disheartening fact dawned upon the adventurous velocipedeist that he had lost all command over his two-wheeler. His first thought was to spring into the first soft place in the road that presented itself, but he discovered that slipping off the vehicle was no easy matter. He therefore determined to keep his seat, and fixing his hat firmly over his brow, he went on helter-skelter to the no little astonishment of the natives of the district.

The inevitable soon occurred. At a sharp bend 'the machine upset' and the rider was 'shot out of his seat like a rocket and left sprawling in the mud'.

It is said [the report concluded] that workmen are now busy building velocipedes in Bacup for their own private use, but with the fate of this unhappy professor of music before their eyes, we shall be very much surprised if they venture on the same road.

Engineering firms also had hopes of the Rossendale market, among them Joseph Webb & Sons, of Bury, who exhibited bicycles and tricycles at the Newchurch Agricultural Show on 29 April. These 'curiosities', said the *Times*, 'attracted a great deal of notice, though we did not hear that they met with purchasers'.

On 5 June, the *Times* reported that two local 'velocipedestrians' had travelled the four miles from Bacup to Rawtenstall in twenty minutes and had later tried to race a train over the same route. At Lee Mill, meanwhile, a group of youths were forming a velocipede club on the co-operative principle with shares at five shillings each.

The same edition of the newspaper revealed that horses disliked the newfangled machines and had attacked at least two of them. In Newchurch Road, a young animal lashed out at a velocipede, causing the rider to swerve into a wall, and at Lee Mill, two Rawtenstall men were kicked from their tandem, which was so badly damaged that it had to be taken to a Bacup foundry for repairs.

The sporting possibilities of the mania soon became apparent. A velocipede race featured in the programme for a gala held on Bacup cricket ground by the Wellington Band. There was only one entry, however, and even this machine failed to put in an appearance because it 'broke its back' before the start of the sports and had to be 'placed in the care of a doctor'. Much more successful were the races at other field days during the summer, most notably the 'Grand Athletic Festival', which attracted 10,000 to Haslingden on 1 July. 'Novel machines of various builds' took part, said the *Haslingden Chronicle*, which noted that in spite of a bumpy course, 'most of the jockeys managed their steeds with great skill' and surprised the watchers with their pace. Among the entries were two four-wheel machines with two riders each. By mid-August, when the Whitewell Vale Agricultural Society organized its first sports, the velocipede race was an accepted attraction. There were, in fact, two races – one fast and one slow. The site of the games, said the *Times*, was a field on the summit of the hill nearly opposite the Roebuck Inn; and to this lofty arena went a man with a four-wheeler. He entered the slow race, at the start of which, however, 'he upset a local celebrity known as "Witt" and both vehicles came to grief'. Though the riders quickly regained their seats, they soon came to 'a dead stand on the rising ground', allowing a Mr Horn from Ramsbottom to take the prize. Mr Horn was something of an expert, for he won the fast race as well, and a week later won again at the Glen Bottom Fair.

The arrival of the velocipedes inspired mechanically-minded Rossendalians not only to copy standard designs, but also to construct wonderful machines of their own. Two Haslingden brothers named Patterson built a tricycle with a front wheel 7ft 6in in diameter and the rear wheels about a foot less. 'Pattersons' Elephant', as it came to be known, accommodated eight passengers seated in two rows, one above the other, behind the steerer. It got out of control on the hill leading into Accrington, ran into a house and was not repaired. Another Haslingden inventor, Richard Barnes ('Dicky Brush') built a four-wheeler which carried four passengers, who were expected to provide most of the motive power by using their hands as well as their feet. The uncertain steering probably explains the machine's demise in a sand hole at Baxenden.

Chapter 21

BRAVO BOTTESINI!

ON TO THE STAGE of the Co-operative Hall, Bacup, on 5 February 1887, walked a famous Italian. At considerable expense, the town's orchestral society had engaged Giovanni Bottesini, friend of Verdi, composer, conductor and one of the few men to have made the double bass a vehicle for breathtaking virtuosity. It was a night to remember. 'A more masterly performance was never witnessed in Bacup. The audience were thoroughly astonished and delighted,' said the *Bacup Times*. 'The perfect control which he exhibited over his monster fiddle was most wonderful.'

> The first note, clear and ringing like that of a violincello, gave evidence of the master touch, and when after the slow and majestic 'Elégie', he came to the spritely 'Tarantella' (both his own works) the audience was held spellbound. He seemed to revel in harmonics of a very high pitch, a great proportion of which were obtained below the end of the fingerboard and within a few inches of the bridge. At the conclusion of the piece a loud round of applause burst out with shouts of 'Bravo! Bravo!'

The 'gem of the evening,' said the *Times*, was the 'Carnival of Venice'. 'It is simply impossible to describe the performance. The variations were given with surprising rapidity and very extraordinary effect. In places the performance had a decidedly comic effect and the audience burst into roars of laughter, which Signor Bottesini could not refrain from joining in. The applause was something terrific.'

In the following October, the Bacup Choral Society, encouraged, perhaps, by the success of Bottesini's visit, engaged Charles Hallé and his wife, the violinist Wilhelmina Norman-Neruda, for a concert in the Mechanics' Institution. The music on this occasion was on a higher level than that performed on the double bass, the A flat piano sonata, Opus 26, of Beethoven proving too advanced for many of the listeners.

Despite a much higher admission price than was usual in Rossendale – reserved seats cost 7s. 6d. – there was 'a large and fashionable audience', including most of the local gentry. The front seats, said the *Times*, were occupied by people in full dress, 'a circumstance which excited a considerable amount of interest'.

As well as the sonata, Hallé played shorter pieces by Schubert, Heller and Chopin, all of which were greeted 'with a tremendous round of applause mingled with cries of "Bravo!" and "Encore!"' The *Times* said the sonata was listened to with rapt attention, but the *Bacup and Rossendale News* considered the performance 'rather too long' since it appeared to weary most of the audience.

In a district where standards were much influenced by brass band music, it was only to be expected that a knowledge of more serious compositions (Handel's much-performed *Messiah* excepted) should be limited. It was not until the invention of the gramophone and the introduction of broadcasting that the musically-inclined were able to acquaint themselves easily with the works of the masters. But some progress was made. Colonel Munn promoted celebrity concerts at Waterfoot in the late '60s, and these were followed on 4 March 1873, by a visit of 'Mr Charles Hallé's Unrivalled Band' to the Co-operative Hall in Rawtenstall. Advertisements advised patrons that 'Special trains will run as follows after the concert: to Bacup and intermediate stations at about 10.30; to Ewood Bridge, Stubbins and Ramsbottom about 10.40'.

> The first-class seats [said the *Times*] were well attended; the second seats moderate and the gallery was nearly filled, but the middle

and back part of the hall was nearly empty. The audience totalled 470 ... and the gentleman who engaged Mr Hallé will lose by this concert at least £40.

To modern eyes, the programme was unusual: The orchestra played the first movement of Beethoven's Pastoral Symphony, three overtures, including Rossini's *William Tell*, the *Rosamunde* ballet music of Schubert and, with Hallé as soloist, an 'electrifying performance' of Mendelsshon's first piano concerto. There were operatic arias from Nita Gaetano, a leading soprano of the day, and a 'grand flute solo, *Il Tremola*, by Mons F. Brosso. Though the pieces were well received, this was the only concert given in Rossendale by a professional orchestra during the nineteenth century. A leading article in the *News* a few months later summed up the cultural scene.

> A company of *artistes* occasionally occupy one of our public halls for a night, but this species of entertainment does not meet with much support. Its success depends upon the class of music or performance, and it is no libel upon the tastes of Rossendale people generally to say that high-class and refined recreation is not appreciated by them.

Shakespeare reached Bacup in March, 1868, when a touring company gave *Othello*, *Macbeth* and *Hamlet* on consecutive nights, but melodramas provided the usual fare. There were limits, however, and *The Era* reported that the Bacup magistrates granted a licence for a portable theatre at Waterfoot only after one member of the bench had 'gravely extracted' from the proprietor 'a promise that the actors would not play *Jack Sheppard* or *Dick Turpin*'.

When operas were performed for the first time in Bacup in 1871, they were followed by farces. The promoters of the English Lyric Opera and Burlesque Company ('Sixteen in number') knew that most of Britain lacked 'high-class and refined recreation' and if audiences were to be introduced to such works as *Il Travatore* and *La Sonnambula*, they would have to be tempted with light-hearted pieces, such as *Prince Amiable*, which made them laugh.

The increase in both affluence and leisure during the later years of the century was reflected in the growth of amateur music making, which saw the opening of shops that sold musical instruments: two in both Rawtenstall and Haslingden and others in Bacup, Stacksteads, Waterfoot and Edenfield. Pianists were particularly numerous, and the demand for new works was so great that at least two local 'professors of music' placed their compositions before the public. From David Wilcock in 1877 came *The Bacup Polka* and *Nellie Waltz*, which were followed a year later by Willie Lord's *Irwell Springs Gallop*. His mazurka, *The Lily*, followed in 1885.

A boy who may have played these pieces when he took his first lessons about this time was Baxter Buckley, of Haslingden. After studying at Waterfoot, Manchester, Leipzig and Berlin, he became a concert pianist, but spent most of his life in New Zealand, where he died in 1920, aged 45.

Several small orchestras formed during the 1870s met with little success. The public appearances of the Stacksteads Philharmonic Society were confined to playing occasionally for the roller-skaters at the new Bacup rink, while an unnamed orchestra trained by Mr Philetas Whittaker, a Haslingden music teacher, is remembered only for the hilarious finale of a concert it gave in Helmshore on behalf of the village band. Before beginning Boildieu's overture to *The Caliph of Baghdad*, the players tuned up to what they believed was an A, struck on the piano by one of their number. Unfortunately it was a much higher note, and the resulting orchestral sound caused wholesale chaos and dismay. The listeners, however, were compensated by the curious antics of a clarinettist who became convinced that a joker had blocked the bell of his instrument. He played a note or two and then held up his clarinet to the light like a telescope. At the end of the piece, the players fled from the platform, knocking the chairman from his seat as they did so.

By the mid 1880s, musical standards had grown sufficiently to prompt the formation in both Bacup and Haslingden of orchestral societies, which frequently engaged soloists of national and occasionally if international rank. The Bacup orchestra began its first concert (in October 1884) with Beethoven's *Prometheus* overture and also gave the allegro from Haydn's 'Surprise' Symphony. The Haslingden Society came before the public in the following year with a selection from *Patience*, though it later embarked from time to time on more demanding works. The andante of Beethoven's First Symphony was well received in 1895, but the inclusion of Wagner's *Tannhauser* overture two years later brought from the *Haslingden Guardian* a plea that 'performances of such difficult and little-understood music should not be too frequent'.

For every Rossendalian who took up a musical instrument, there were many more who joined either a church choir or one of the choral societies which came and went during the nineteenth century. The accomplishments of the Dean Layrocks, who turned their loom shops into music shops, as one of them put it, have often been recorded. They knew by heart many of the masterpieces of Handel, Haydn and Mozart, and passed on their love of these works to others. Charles Hallé praised the fine singing of the Bacup Choral Society when he shared a platform with its members in 1887. Seven years later the town's Temperance Choir won first prize at the Co-operative Contest in the Crystal Palace.

> I found, as I had anticipated, that the choir is entirely made up of millworkers [wrote Dr Spencer Curwen in the October issue of the *Musical Herald*]. The conductor, Mr Charles Hollows, is an overseer of looms in a mill, and like his singers, works from 6am to 5.30pm. The choir numbers 42 and rehearses twice a week. The applicant for membership is admitted on probation. He or she attends practice for a week or two; and if the members think they have a recruit likely to be a strength to the choir, they vote him or her in. As nearly all the members belong to the Bacup Choral Society and to a church or chapel choir, many of them rehearse four nights a week! Of all the places of worship in Bacup (20 or 30), Mr Hollows can remember only one which has not a choirmaster as well as an organist. The Bacup children go to work in the mills (as half-timers) at eleven and they work on till old age lays them aside. It is a town of toilers. All the more reason to rejoice that the

love of music among the people is so keen. They turn to the art with a zest that only busy people can know.

People of all musical tastes – and many with none at all – were brought together in December, 1890, when Edison's 'wonderful talking machine' was demonstrated in the Valley. A 'crowded audience' in the Bacup Mechanics' Institution enjoyed 'an intellectual treat' as the 'phonograph gave off its impressions in a perfectly delightful style', said the *Rossendale Division Gazette*. During the evening, 'the Irwell Springs Band played selections into the instrument in a clever manner and the sounds were reproduced by the phonograph with beautiful correctness'.

Gilbert and Sullivan's light operas were given in the Royal Court Theatre in Bacup by D'Oyly Carte touring companies in both 1894 and 1896, though on the first visit, according to the *Gazette*, 'the audience was far from satisfactory considering the expensiveness of the engagement'. Perhaps comfort was a factor, for the advertisements for the 1896 productions of *The Mikado* and *The Gondoliers* included an 'Important notice', informing would-be patrons that 'The theatre is now thoroughly warm, cosy and free from draughts'.

Bacup, in February, 1896, also heard a piano recital by Leonard Borwick, described as 'England's greatest pianist'. The programme included Beethoven's 'Les Adieux' sonata and a popular piece by an up and coming young Russian – the Prelude in C Sharp Minor, by Rachmaninov. The concert was arranged on behalf of the Rossendale Society for the Blind by Mrs J. H. Maden, whose husband, one of Lancashire's leading 'cotton lords', was probably the richest man in Rossendale. It was to the couple's love of music and good works that the Valley owed its greatest cultural 'scoop'. The story is told in the next chapter.

Chapter 22

THE QUEEN OF SONG

EVEN TODAY IT SEEMS REMARKABLE, but in 1911 it was a sensation. It was if it had been announced that the FA Cup Final would be played at Waterfoot or Whitewell Bottom. Dame Nellie Melba – the most celebrated singer of her day – was to visit Bacup.

Melba commanded enormous fees, the sort that only cities the size of London, Paris and New York could afford, but there was brass in Bacup, too. Quite a few fortunes had been made there and now and then the 'cottonocracy' liked a 'bit of a do'. And so it was in 1911, when the Mayor and Mayoress, Alderman and Mrs J. H. Maden decided to raise money for the Bacup Sick Nursing Society by engaging 'The World's Queen of Song' herself.

When Melba accepted the engagement, many people believed the concert would never take place. To some the idea seemed preposterous; and as 6 February drew near, the whole town was in suspense as rumours about the singer's health and her unwillingness to venture into darkest Lancashire grew stronger.

At length, as the *Bacup Times* put it, 'special inquiries were set on foot' and a telegram was sent to Melba in Paris. To everyone's relief came the reassuring reply: 'There is positively no ground for alarm. The concert will go on'.

Tickets went on sale three weeks before the big day, with the best seats costing a guinea, which was more than a week's pay for many local people. Demand was brisk, however.

The plan for the higher-priced seats opened on Monday forenoon, but applicants were waiting as early as ten minutes past eight, and within half an hour of the opening of the plan, close on a hundred of the guinea and half-guinea tickets had been disposed of. One of the earliest applicants secured fifty two of the half-guinea for himself and a party, and another applicant placed an order for twelve. On Wednesday, when the five shilling tickets were offered for sale, there was another big rush.

When the time came to buy the half crown tickets a queue formed several hours before the box office opened, and again there was a rapid sell-out. A number of local people earned extra spending money by keeping places in the line. Others arrived with their pockets stuffed with coins. One of the first to arrive had a commission to buy half crown tickets for the whole of Weir Terrace.

Once the wider world accepted that Bacup really had achieved a musical scoop, requests for tickets came from as far as London. The cheapest, however, were strictly rationed. 'The Mayor and Mayoress have stipulated that the whole of the upper gallery, with the exception of the front row, shall be devoted to sixpenny seats. They have further stipulated that tickets shall only be sold to householders in Bacup and no one householder shall have more than two'.

Not surprisingly, the next edition of the local paper carried the following announcement on its front page:

> SPECIAL NOTICE: The demand for 2*s*. 6*d*. seats having been so much greater than the supply, it has been decided to erect a Special Staging behind the Family Circle, which will provide standing room for several hundred persons; this special stand will be so arranged that all persons of medium height should be able to see the stage. Tickets for this standing room are now on sale at 2*s*. 6*d*. each.

The Melba concert was almost the sole topic of conversation in Bacup. Was the famous singer really coming? To some it seemed like a dream and even the organizers began to have their doubts again. Off went another telegram and once more came the reassuring reply: 'Melba is absolutely certain to appear'.

And so to the great day. From early morning an army of men and women worked on decorating the theatre; and the mayor's own gardener and his staff crafted on the stage 'a great mound of plants and foliage eight to ten feet high at the wings and gradually declining to floor level, where it bordered a sort of pathway leading to a French window at the back of the setting'.

There was a red carpet, of course, and also a specially-constructed passage leading from the stage door to the point where Melba and the other performers were due to step down from their carriages. This was 'the open space opposite the Corporation store yard', but since it was dark when the carriages drew up, it is unlikely that anyone noticed.

To reach Rossendale, Melba and her party travelled by a special train. It was due to arrive at 7.10, but pulled into Bacup station at half past six, causing much consternation. 'As a consequence,' said the *Times*, 'the party had to be accommodated in the station-master's office until the carriages could be telephoned for'.

What the great soprano thought of this is not recorded, but she is said to have been thrilled with her room at the theatre, which had been 'beautifully trimmed with linen and lace'.

The concert itself – there were four other artists – lasted two hours and raised £272 13*s*. 6*d*. for the Nursing Society. Melba sang *Se Saren Rose* by Arditi, *The Jewel Song* from *Faust* and Tosti's *Goodbye*. There were encores, of course – *Down in the Forest, Comin' through the Rye* and finally *Home, sweet home* to her own accompaniment at the piano.

'The audience was loath to let her go,' said the *Times*, 'They re-called her again and again, and on her last appearance she brought onto the stage a great handful of magnificent flowers, which she distributed among the people. Then, throwing kisses to the cheering throng, she was gone'.

Chapter 23

THE MUSICAL MILL MASTER

ON 5 SEPTEMBER 1864, six working men from Weir were at the Belle Vue, Manchester, brass band contest, when the band of the 4th Lancashire Rifle Volunteers, which had been formed and equipped by its commanding officer, Robert Munn, gained the first prize. As we shall see in the next chapter, the triumph had far-reaching consequences.

Munn, a leading figure in the Bacup cotton trade, was a gifted musician, who was organist and choirmaster at St James's Church in Waterfoot, where the congregation often heard his compositions alongside those of Handel, Haydn, Mozart, Weber and other masters. Several of his songs have come down to us, but the woks he composed for his band appear to have been lost.

When Britain's strained relations with France led the Government, in 1859, to recruit a volunteer militia, there was a rush to arms throughout the country. Munn was the second officer in England to be commissioned, the 4th LRV having been formed only ten days after General Peel, the Secretary of State for War, made his case for action. Within a matter of weeks, Munn provided his 87 recruits not only with the first paid drill instructor and the first fully-equipped rifle range in England, but also with splendid uniforms of silver grey and scarlet. The *Bury Times* of 23 July reported:

On Saturday last, the 4th LRV assembled at the Commercial Hotel in their new uniforms under the command of Captain Munn. There were 3,000 spectators to witness, in an adjoining field, the military evolutions of the corps.

Munn also recruited the Broadclough Band and placed it in the care of George Ellis, of Blackburn, the leading brass musician of the day. 'Your instruction and your counsel,' the players told their tutor in a testimonial some six years later, 'enabled us to carry the palm of victory from an assemblage of the most celebrated bands in the country'.

This was a reference to, among other successes, the 4th LRV's first triumph at Belle Vue – a day on which more than 2,000 supporters travelled to Manchester in special trains and on which many times that number thronged the streets of Bacup to welcome back the champions.

'The judges had no difficulty in awarding the First Prize of £30,' said the *Manchester Times*, adding that the 4th LRV 'seemed to be the favourites' and that the result was greeted by 'a loud outburst of applause which continued for some time'. The test piece was *The Reminiscences of Auber*.

It was after midnight when the twenty members of the band returned, wrote Isaac Leach, the band's historian, but the whole of the town's inhabitants were awaiting their arrival. Along Newchurch Road the band played *John Brown's Body* and the crowds, thousands in number, joined in the strains.

In the following year, the band supported by even greater numbers, again won the Belle Vue championship, and the enthusiasm as they walked through the streets from the railway station at midnight 'could not have been surpassed if they had been a victorious army returning from the wars'.

Thereafter, the band was rarely out of the news. In nine years it competed in forty eight contests, winning thirty three first prizes – thirteen in succession – and returning empty-handed only once.

Test pieces were usually arrangements of themes from well-known operas, *William Tell*, *Faust*, *Maritana*, *Der Freischutz* and so on, but lighter music, some by Munn himself, was also in the band's repertoire. On a cold afternoon in October, 1864, when the Volunteers held a shooting match on the Intack Range in Stacksteads, Mozart and Munn (now a lieutenant colonel) again came together, the commanding officer contributing a waltz, *Vectis*, and *The Lancashire Galop* to a programme which ended with the overture to *The Magic Flute*.

To hear music performed by instrumentalists he had helped to raise to a position of pre-eminence, was a pleasure Munn, along with many Rossendalians, regularly enjoyed. The band played at his fund-raising functions and at least once for his workpeople. The *Bacup and Rossendale News* of 29 September 1866, noted:

> On Saturday last, Colonel Munn treated upwards of 600 of his hands to Blackpool. They were accompanied by the Rifle Band and enjoyed themselves famously. Those who preferred to stay at home were paid their day's wages. Such generosity might be followed with advantage by other employers of labour in Rossendale.

Munn delighted in 'opening' any new organ in the locality, even at Baptist and Unitarian chapels, and also in bringing to Rossendale some of the best professional singers and instrumentalists in the North of England. The programme for one of his 'grand fashionable concerts' given at Waterfoot in 1867, included Beethoven's 'Pathetique' piano sonata and a two-piano arrangement of Mendelssohn's Scottish Symphony. For another in the same year, Munn hired 'Broadwood's full grand piano as used at the leading Manchester concerts'. On it were played selections from *Martha* and *La Traviata*.

There was also 'R. M. Junior', the composer of salon music. *The Grasmere Gallop* and two songs are in the British Library, and an illustrated cover of *The Rossendale Hunt Gallop* is the Whitaker Park Museum. Other pieces are known only from newspaper references.

Like many second generation industrialists, Munn had no desire to devote his entire life to commerce. He rode regularly with the Rossendale Hunt, served as a magistrate and busied himself philanthropically in the social, religious and political life of the district. He calculated that from 1858 to 1869 he spent on good causes no less than £44,000, much of it during the Cotton Famine, when he not only contributed magnanimously to the Relief Fund, but also maintained a soup kitchen at Waterfoot and paid unemployed men to lay out the extensive grounds of his home, Thistle Mount at Newchurch. It was there in happier times that he gave house parties of a kind never previously known in Rossendale. The 'scale of splendour' and Munn's 'unbounded hospitality' were still remembered more than fifty years later, when the *Free Press* collected material for his obituary.

The playing of the Volunteers' band on these glittering occasions was always much admired, and Munn himself recalled, that 'monarchs in their castle yards or grounds' never heard sweeter music than that performed on the lawn at Thistle Mount.

When only thirty two, Munn, left the Valley to become a cotton broker in Liverpool and composed there a song he called *A Memory* and dedicated it to the Countess of Sefton. The *Daily Post* wrote of its 'special charm and quaintness' and thought it was 'in every way prettily conceived and worked out'. The review of this and four other songs appeared at the beginning of February, 1876. Less than a month later Munn's name was in almost every newspaper in Lancashire. He had failed to appear before the city magistrates to answer a charge of fraudulently conspiring with a business partner to obtain 600 bales of cotton. Munn had fled to Spain and nothing more was heard of him in Rossendale until 1902, when he was interviewed by a representative of the *Bacup Times* while staying with his son, the Rev. J. T. Munn, vicar from 1896 until 1908 of St James's, Waterfoot, the church he had paid for.

Munn, once the most popular man in Rossendale, died in London in 1906, leaving £52 17*s*. 9*d*.

Chapter 24

'THE PINNACLE OF FAME'

COLONEL MUNN LIVED JUST LONG ENOUGH to see a second Rossendale band, Irwell Springs, take its place alongside the very best, though whether or not he realised that he was indirectly responsible for its formation in 1864, it is impossible to say. The Rifle Volunteers' success at Belle Vue inspired the six men who were at the contest to form a band in their own village.

'We determined,' they announced in a circular, 'that our little village shall have something to enliven it;' and a laconic entry in the minute book sums up the pioneering spirit:

Name: *L. Hey.*

Choice of instrument: *Aught*

The band held its first practice in a bedroom with a bedstead serving as a bandstand.

The standard of playing in the early years gave no hint at the triumphs to come. When Springs competed at Whitworth in 1877, the judge said of the performance:

Opened out of tune; tenor horns and second cornets very much out of tune; very bad precision; solo cornet did not play very well; little running passages very imperfect; rarely well balanced.

It was not until the engagement in 1896 of the celebrated bandsman William Rimmer (1861–1936) that the villagers began to grow into a formidable contesting force. Rimmer did for Springs what George Ellis had done for the 4th LRV more than thirty years previously: he transformed a group of amateur musicians, all of them artisans, into national champions.

The faith in the players' potential by the seventeen local men who paid the director's fee was soon justified, and progress was so good that by 1901, the band was able to compete in the top section of the National Brass Band Championship in London. For the competition, which began in the previous year, Sir Arthur Sullivan and his fellow directors of the Crystal Palace provided a Thousand Guinea Trophy. This glittering prize was exhibited throughout the country and reached Bacup on 4 September 1901, when it was on view during a concert given by the band in the Mechanics' Institution, The *Bacup Times* reported

> The trophy arrived by the four o'clock train in the charge of Mr J. H. Isles, the director of the Crystal Palace contest, and two assistants, It was contained in a large iron-bound chest and was taken in a hand cart directly to the Queen's Hotel until the time of the exhibition in the evening ... During the interval of the concert, the audience was given an opportunity of a closer examination of the cup, being allowed to pass round the table on which it was exhibited. The trophy is most magnificent. It is of superb design and of the finest workmanship. It is composed of solid gold and silver and encrusted with numerous gems,

The contest took place at the end of the month, the Bacup players travelling overnight to London after a final rehearsal of the test piece, *Gems from Sullivan's Operas*. At the Crystal Palace, the band, in the words of the *Times*, 'played in exquisite style and with such delicacy and expression as to instantly gain the attention of the vast audience'.

> Springs were placed second, only two points behind the winners, Lee Mount, and a rousing welcome would have been theirs had they returned home on any day but Sunday. 'With the exception of a subdued cheer that the large crowd waiting at the station

could not suppress, there was no demonstration whatsoever. The people in the streets, despite the enthusiasm that was in them, remembered the day and refrained in a manner to be commended from giving way to their feelings in loud shouting or cheers.

Things were different in 1905, when Springs won contests in Nelson, Darwen and Southport before going on to take the 'Open' at Belle Vue. Would they now become the first band to win both the Belle Vue and the Crystal Palace contests in a single year? The 'huge crowd of loyal enthusiasts' who went to Bacup station to give the players 'a send-off worthy of a victorious MP', had no doubt about the outcome, though the waiting placed a severe strain on their nerves.

The bandsmen left by the 9.57pm train and travelled to London via Rosegrove, Halifax and Wakefield on the Great Northern Line. The journey lasted nine hours; and as the players tried to snatch a little sleep in the crowded compartments, each of them, as the *Times* put it, 'was impressed with the responsibility resting upon him – the responsibility that at home 20,000 people were looking to him to surpass anything previously known'.

After being given breakfast by Hawkes, the musical instrument makers, the players went to a school for a final rehearsal of the test piece, *Roland a Ronceveux* by Auguste Mermet. Only then did they 'proceed to the huge palace of pleasure where the great battle of brass was to take place'.

Though the contest began at noon, it was not until four o'clock that Springs, who played seventeenth out of twenty four, took the stage. 'What anyone who listened to the various bands could not fail to observe,' said the *Times*, 'was the superior quality of tone possessed by Springs over all their competitors'.

> Immediately the band opened, it was noticeable that they were accomplishing something, which no preceding had accomplished – they were playing the unisons which form the selection dead in tune. As they opened, so they progressed right to the end. When the conductor's baton fell on the final note, there was a great

outburst of applause and as the men came off the stage there was a rush to congratulate them.

About fifty Bacupians were at the Crystal Palace; in the town centre many times that number gathered to await the first of two telegrams sent by the *Times* reporter and posted in the window of Mr L. J. Priestly's stationary shop in St James's Street. It arrived shortly before seven o'clock and read:

> Springs gave splendid performance and opinion is that they are 'on top'. Tone was fine and dead in tune, and only two minor slips were made. Band received magnificent ovation. Men are perfectly satisfied with performance and expecting another big success.

Because of a concert by all the bands, it was after nine o'clock when Mr Iles broke the seal on the tin box containing the judges' verdict. The winners of the junior sections came first, adding to the tension among those who waited for the principal result. At length Mr Isles took out the last envelope and slowly began to read: 'Championship Section. First prize – Number Sevent–' Before the word was complete

> A great shout came from the right-hand side of the platform – a shout which was taken up in the stalls and at the sides and at the rear wherever Rossendalians were scattered. For near three minutes the Springs men on the platform kept their lungs going; they beat the air with their caps; they hugged each other and danced, waved their instruments above their heads and generally behaved as if they were hugely pleased with themselves. When it was at all possible, Mr Isles proceeded: 'Number Seventeen – Irwell Springs.' And then the demonstration was renewed, and hundreds of the audience who had not known which band played seventeenth, were unrestrained in their applause ... Mr Isles expressed his delight at the decision and Mr Rimmer was almost too overcome to give expression to his feelings.

'When the news was flashed along the wires that Springs had got first, people went almost wild,' said the *Times* 'There was no other subject talked of … Wherever one went, it was all Springs. Their success seemed to electrify everybody.'

The band had an engagement in London on the day after the contest and did not leave the city until Monday afternoon. News of their arrival at Accrington shortly after nine o'clock was telephoned to Bacup and posted in the window of Mr Priestley's shop. Within minutes it was carried in every direction. From Accrington, the bandsmen, who were joined by their wives and sweethearts, travelled triumphantly to the Valley in two wagonettes. Large crowds greeted them in Haslingden, Rawtenstall and Waterfoot. But, as the *Times* noted,

> The crowning point was yet to come; and the scenes which followed will live in memory as long as life itself. No football team bringing home the English Cup, no general coming home from war, no politician, no, not even General Booth with all his experiences, could have been greeted with a more wild yet fervent outburst of enthusiasm.

After being welcomed in the Thrutch by the Mayor, Alderman J. H. Maden, the procession moved slowly towards the town centre.

> The crowd at Stacksteads Station was enormous, and cheer after cheer rent the air. It was a great demonstration in every sense of the word. There was no pomp, no undue show. But there was a genuineness that could not hide itself, and when at length the band broke forth with 'See the Conquering Hero Comes', the crowd took up the refrain and sang away until they must have been hoarse. Every man, woman and child in Stacksteads seemed to have turned out to greet their heroes, and the bandsmen were touched to the quick by the cordiality with which they were received. Every point of vantage from the Commercial Hotel in Stacksteads to the Swan Hotel at Bacup was occupied, but it was perhaps at the latter place where the crowd was most thickly congested.

> Commencing at the Swan and proceeding to the Working Men's Club, it was one huge mass of people and thousands of throats hoarsely bade their favourites welcome home. They surged in from

of the leading wagonette; and from every window flags and hats were waved.

The bandsmen were cheered all the way to Holmes Villa, where they were received by their President, Mr Abraham Shepherd. They played for him, 'See the Conquering Hero Comes', 'Home, Sweet Home', and 'Auld Lang Syne'.

All copies of the *Rossendale Express*, which carried a full report of the triumph, were rapidly sold. A second edition was printed and still the demand was unsatisfied. The report was then reprinted in the *Bacup Times* of 7 October. It began

> In England's greatest pleasure dome, 70,000 people on Saturday witnessed the raising of the name of Bacup to the very pinnacle of fame in the British brass band world. At the Crystal Palace, London, in the great National Brass Band Contest, Irwell Springs won the thousand guinea championship, the blue riband of brass band contesting, in competition with all comers. Bravo Springs. Bravo William Rimmer, the gentleman who so nobly led them on to victory. What a magnificent end to a season crammed with success. What an honour to a town which from its coal mines and its quarries and its factories can produce such masters of time and tune and technique.

As national champions, Springs were in great demand, and in 1906 undertook an exhausting month-long tour of the South Coast holiday resorts. This left them with little time for contest work and probably explains their decline to seventh place at Crystal Palace. The band did not compete in the following year, but were among the seventeen which competed in 1908, when the test piece was an arrangement of themes from Wagner's *Rienzi*. On the afternoon of the contest, St James' Street was well-filled with townspeople awaiting the first telegram from the *Times* reporter. It arrived at 2.50 and was at once displayed in the window of Mr Priestley's shop.

Irwell Springs played third and have just come off the stage. A tip-top performance. They received a great ovation. Players are highly satisfied and have great hopes of success.

The news encouraged even vaster crowds to gather as the expected time of the result drew near.

Then, at 9.15, there was a movement in the shop and word spread the second telegram was about to be posted.

Every eye, from all angles of vision, was fixed upon that fateful pane. So eager, so expectant, so intensely absorbing was the emotion that it was well nigh to bursting point. The message read:

Irwell Springs – First Prize.

Hurrying feet bore the 'glad tidings of great joy' to other parts of the borough. The crowded house of the Animated Pictures, though in the midst of a serious theme, broke into a wild ferment of jubilation at the announcement, and cheer after cheer suspended for a time all further progress, while at the Theatre similar scenes were enacted. For hours the streets were alive with crowds eagerly discussing the splendid achievement.

By their victory, Springs joined Wingates Temperance in having twice won the Thousand Guinea Trophy. Could they win it a third time and become the first players to receive gold medals? The competition was growing stronger every year, not least from subsidized works bands such as Foden's (the steam wagon company) and Crosfield's Perfection Soap. The resignation of William Rimmer in 1909 – he became full-time director of the municipal band in his home town of Southport – was a serious setback, but both in 1910, guided by the veteran tutor Alex Owen, and 1912 with the rising conductor William Helliwell to direct them, Springs gained second place.

Among the listeners in 1912 was Ruggero Leoncavallo, the composer of *Pagliacci*. 'I do not know how the piece could be better played,' he was reported to have said of Springs' performance of the test piece, William Rimmer's arrangement of themes from Rossini's *William Tell*.

Leoncavallo was one of the few composers of 'serious' music to take an interest in brass bands. Contests, so relished by the working classes, were, generally speaking, regarded with condescension by musicians whose skills lay elsewhere. To one Victorian critic, the popular competitions were 'musical prize fights', and as late as 1912, the *Manchester Guardian*, in its report of the Belle Vue contest, said 'The usages of the music hall and of the sporting field were observed rather than those of the concert hall'.

> There is not much applause at the conclusion of the music, but a prominent request for silence during the course of the selections was not effectual in stopping the recognition of any fine bit of playing on the instant.

It is most interesting, therefore, to find an account of the National Championship of 1913 by Joseph Holbrooke, a leading British composer of both instrumental and chamber music.

> When I decided to attend the Crystal Palace to listen to some brass band playing, I was considerably amused, first with myself and then with my friends, who had the joke well rubbed into me that I should repent it to my dying day, and probably to be sick in bed after it for life. But these fancies I faced stubbornly.
>
> Something has to be done for splendid enthusiasms, and when one appears, we do our level best to find out what it is all about. So it was. I sallied forth many miles and arrived at the seething cauldron of action, to meet brass, tons of brass, handled by honest men of toil. The despised ones! Perhaps if I say outright that I haven astonished in a powerful degree, it will save much time ... for such tone and expression is not found in our bloated string bands of the Queen's Hall or London Symphony calibre. I make safe to say that we have not such brass in quality and fire in London bands at all. Not all are the first excellence, but after one or two bands had tackled quite ably the well-written fantasie by Mr Percy Fletcher, I had a treat, for the Irwell Springs Band (wherever that is) gave a beautiful performance and, indeed, despised the difficulties put up

for them. It was plain to see they despised the chromatic scales and cadenzas and looked round hungrily for more arpeggios and more modulation! With coats off and hair well cropped, we had nothing but genuine effort and every ounce put into it.

Holbrooke's pleasure was shared by the three judges, one of whom was Percy Fletcher himself. He said after hearing Springs play his tone poem, *Labour and Love* – the first test piece to be written for a contest – 'An inspiring performance with which I was delighted in every way'.

When it was announced that the band had beaten twenty one others,

> The bandsmen threw up their caps and their instrument bags, and indulged in strange, but pardonable, methods of jubilation. They danced, they shouted uproariously and even embraced each other. The merry band of supporters too made themselves hoarse with repeated cries, and truly the joy of all Bacup knew no bounds.

In the town itself, people were gathering in such large numbers that soon both sides of St James Street 'as far as the eye could reach' were so crowded that traffic could move only with the greatest difficulty. 'As ten o'clock drew near,' said the *Times*, 'the excitement was at fever heat, and when, five minutes after the hour, the fateful message "Springs first" was posted in the window, there was a delirious outburst of jubilation.'

The band remained in London until Monday in order to make a gramophone record of *Labour and Love* and then travelled to Rawtenstall, where they were met by 'a spacious char-a-banc' drawn by four horses. Greeted everywhere by huge crowds, the players drove first to Leabank Hall, home of the Mayor of Bacup, Col. J. Craven Hoyle; and, after numerous stops, to their headquarters at the Green Man. Of the triumphant tour, the *Times* columnist observed,

> I do not think the streets of Bacup have ever been more closely packed ... The swaying, surging mass on Bull's Head Bridge was unparalleled in the history of the town ... Veritably, all Rossendale was agog with enthusiasm.

Chapter 25

Practice makes perfect

The villagers of Irwell Springs were by no means alone in their love of music. Those in Goodshawfold collected enough money in 1867 to buy some old instruments, which a kindly local tinsmith put into working order. The bandsmen practised for several months in a cellar until they worked up enough confidence to march through the streets.

> Every inhabitant turned out to discover what the funny noise was [one of the players recalled in later life] and when they found it was the band, there was such jubilation as had never occurred in the fold before. Home-brewed ale was brought out and seemed to put courage into the bandsmen. A few weeks later, the band went on Hameldon Moor for the next attempt to play a march. All the fold residents went with them. On striking up, horses, cattle, sheep and wild animals flew in terror. I never could tell which made the most noise – the band or the animals.

Undeterred by this inauspicious baptism, the determined men practised even harder, grew more and accomplished and in 1869 Goodshaw Band won fourth prize at a contest in Colne. In both 1905 and 1906, they came fifth in the National Championship at the Crystal Palace, and in the following year were second. The silver Workington Cup, won in 1906, '07 and '08, is in the Whitaker Museum.

Each summer, Rossendale towns and villages staged contests of their own, drawing competitors from all parts of the North. These were splendid Saturdays of intense excitement and carnival gaiety, when even the cotton masters were known to close their factories.

The early visitor to Bacup on 15 August 1868 would have seen sixteen boys 'dressed in fantastic colours' and drawing a rushcart adorned with musical instruments and kitchen utensils. These doffers from Shepherd's mill were keen to outshine their opposite numbers from the mill of Smith and Sons. Rushcart No, 2, when it appeared later in the morning, was a good match for its rival. Evergreens and copper kettles provided the decoration, and a placard read 'May the best band win the first prize'. Its young attendants 'wore long white stockings with knickerbocker trousers secured by coloured ribbons' and sported crowns of coloured paper.

Throughout the morning, special trains, each crowded with supporters, steamed into the station, from which the bands marched to their quarters playing lively airs. Promptly at one o'clock, to the cheers of 10,000 followers, the eight competing bands paraded up Market Street to the contest ground overlooking the town. There the instruments to be given as prizes were suspended from a cross beam and were much admired.

Throughout the sunny afternoon and until seven in the evening the bands played selections arranged from well-known operas, after which individual players competed for a four-valve euphonium, a tenor horn and a soprano cornet. The winning band, Matlock, received £30 and a bass drum (new skeleton model) worth fourteen guineas and ended the contest 'by playing their prize air amidst great cheering'.

Chapter 26

ARCTIC FOOTBALL

THE HAMLET OF IRWELL SPRINGS produced not only a famous brass band, but also a football team, which was better than most until professionalism led to the rise of the big town and city clubs. The village lads were good enough to beat Burnley 4–0 in 1881 and to take on Bolton Wanderers five years later. This third round tie in the Lancashire Cup competition was the most extraordinary ever seen in the Valley (or most other places, for that matter) since it was played throughout in a blizzard.

Snow began to fall on the Broadclough ground at eleven o'clock in the morning of 14 December and by the starting time there were drifts of more than a foot and a general covering of at least four inches. In spite of these Arctic conditions, there was a good crowd to cheer on the home side, who kicked off with what the *Bacup Times* described as a strong gale behind them.

Springs scored after ten minutes and 'during the rest of the first half play was nearly all in front of the Wanderers' goal. Corners and goal kicks occurred every few minutes, but owing to the faultless defence of the goalkeeper, no second goal could be made.'

> At half time, the game stood at one goal to nil in favour of Springs, but immediately on change of ends, the tables were turned. The home team began to play in a defensive manner, but the visitors were too powerful for them and in four minutes Bullough scored the first

goal for Wanderers. A minute later, Cook (Springs' keeper) allowed a very easy shot by Struthers to cross the line, but the blinding snow in his face made it almost impossible to for him to see the ball, besides the snow being drifted about a foot deep in front of the goal. Two minutes later he allowed another easy shot by Struthers to go through his legs and a minute later Hewitson put a fourth through. It was evident that the Springs had not the slightest chance as the terrific wind blowing down the field made it next to impossible to make any headway against it, and after eight minutes' play they gave up the game, which was the most sensible thing they could do.

A group of Scotsmen, who took jobs at the Irwell Springs Dyeworks, introduced Association Football into the district during the 1870s. Their informal games attracted the local lads, in particular J. W. (Jack) Taylor, who recruited a team which beat the 'foreigners' on Christmas Day, 1877. The following year saw the formation of the village club, the members contributing half a crown each to buy orange and black cross-striped jerseys, black knickers and matching black caps. The club rules forbade swearing and abusive language during games and also required the players to pay their own expenses. Looking back to those times, Mr Taylor remembered that

> The same pair of shoes generally did duty for football and Sunday alike. The players used to go every Sunday morning to Doals or Heald Sunday schools with the leather bars still across the bottoms of their shoes.

At this time, the association game was overshadowed by rugby – there were 27 rugby clubs in Bacup alone – but after the start of the Rossendale Charity Competition in 1884, it became enormously popular. Springs were the first winners, though it required a semi-final replay and two replays of the final to settle the matter. These games raised £170, which was used to buy a cup for future winners.

Springs were now a power in the football world and, as Mr Taylor recalled, 'People travelled from all parts of Lancashire to see the excellent passing and dodging for which Dennis Howarth and John Rankin had become famous.' Before referees took charge of matches, two linesmen, known as umpires, settled points of dispute. Springs had an umpire called Jonas Cronshaw, who would often rush across the field to his opposite number and emphasise his claim with that never-to-be-forgotten walking stick in a manner which could not be resisted.

Opponents in the 1880s included Renton, holders of the Scottish Association Cup, and Oswestry. In April, 1885, a crowd of more than 2,500, watched Springs go down 3–1 to the Scotsmen at Old Meadows, but on Good Friday of the following year, the villagers beat Oswestry, who had five Welsh internationals, 4–0. The Springs goalkeeper was reported to have touched the ball only once during the second half. By 1888, the local cup final was of sufficient standing to merit a visit by 'Free Critic' of the *Athletic News*, who had as much to say about the landscape and its people as the game itself.

> When the Great Architect of the Universe made the plans of the world, he marked one spot and called it the Valley of Rossendale, for it is written, 'Behold, I will make a valley, the like of which will not be equalled, and it shall be called the Valley of Rossendale. At the bottom shall be left space sufficient for the construction of a brook, a turnpike road and a railway, and on the sides shall be built houses of stone, which shall be peopled by people of excitable temperaments, and houses of wood, which shall be inhabited by the feathered tribe and the tribe of swine. And on the tops thereof shall men of the common herd disport themselves at ye game of football. And it was done, and is so to this day. The railway has scarcely sufficient space to secure its usual width, and in many places, where has been a load or two slipped in by mistake, they have to resort to tunnels. The houses are built on the sides of the hills, and so far as I know, all the football grounds are on top of the hills, with a streamer to denote their whereabouts to the stranger at the bottom. Each householder considers it part of his furnishings to invest in a wooden erection and stock it with hens or pigs. There are hundreds of them between Ramsbottom and Bacup. Another peculiarity of the inhabitants of this benighted district is a general habit of walking about with both hands rammed down in the breeches pockets.

I'll guarantee that out of twenty persons you meet, nineteen will be strutting away or standing still in this fashion, and it must be hereditary, for I met a hale old gentleman of about seventy coming down the hill leading to the football ground with a bucket on one arm and both hands in his pockets, with a bucket bobbing about in a rather uncomfortable manner. That's the Valley of Rossendale explained, but not moralised.

The match on Saturday was the event of the season, for it was none other than the annual fight in the final tie for the local Charity Cup, a cup much valued among Rossendalians. The contending teams were Irwell Springs and Rawtenstall, and the match was well attended, 4,000 strong-lunged hen-keepers mounting the hill to the Dark Lane enclosure. I noticed that the Rossendale club has erected a stand, which Mr Hall, the secretary, informed me was the best in the Valley. It is a good one, and substantial, as it needs to be to hold its own against the Rossendale winds. It was unfortunate for Rawtenstall that they lost one of their men when half-an-hour had expired, for it takes all the go out of the others; but at the same time, I do not think they could have won, and I consider Irwell Springs as the best team, though it would have been a much closer finish than four to one.

The Lancashire Cup competition, which kicked off in 1878, attracted church and village teams as well as clubs that joined the Football League on its formation in 1888. Cloughfold, Rossendale, Rawtenstall, Water, Stacksteads Working Men, Haslingden Church Institute and Haslingden Grane tried their luck, often briefly, but Springs took part, with mixed fortunes, from the 1880–81 to 1890–91. In 1890, they beat Manchester (one of the several teams in the city) 19–0, a record which still stands. They then lost 11–1 to Blackburn Rovers, already four times winners of the FA Cup and winners again in this season and the next. Having beaten Turton 2–1 two years previously, Springs held the Rovers to a 1–1 draw, but lost 5–1 in the replay at Blackburn.

Chapter 27

GENTLEMEN AND PLAYERS

CRICKET THRIVED PRODIGIOUSLY in Rossendale as the nineteenth century brought changing attitudes, prosperity and much greater leisure. The game, which the Primitive Methodists of Haslingden denounced in 1832 as 'contrary to the Word of God', was promoted on two fronts – by the men, who founded the leading clubs, and by numerous teams of villagers, tradesmen, mill workers and even Bible classes.

Alongside the workingmen's games played on street corners, rough ground and sloping meadows, there blossomed at a higher social level club cricket, from which for a time artisans took no part. The founders of the Haslingden club in 1853 had much in common besides an interest in sport. They had been educated at public or grammar schools; they were, with one or two exceptions, members of the Church of England; in politics, they were mostly Conservatives; and above all, they described themselves as gentlemen. In the 1850s, only gentlemen (meaning here the local gentry) had the time and money to take part in organised games, which were often arranged for weekdays. Mill owners, land owners and professional men made up the first teams to play on the Bentgate ground, and it was said that almost every player came in his own carriage. On match days 'there were often a score of conveyances in Private Lane'.

'Pure and wholesome cricket' was ensured – indeed, enforced – by strict rules, of which even the Primitive Methodists would have approved. Meetings in licensed premises were forbidden and 'no match shall be played amongst members for a wager, however trivial, members simply restricting themselves to the honour got'. Fines, which were widely used in mills, friendly societies and even in chapels, had their place at the cricket club.

> Any player absenting himself from the field on three successive Saturdays without giving a just reason for so doing to the satisfaction of the committee – 1s.
>
> Any member absenting himself from the general meeting without giving a written and satisfactory notice to the secretary previous to the meeting – 6d.
>
> Any member swearing – 1s.

Mrs John Townsend, whose husband and father were founders of the club, recalled that for their first match, the players wore white trousers with blue stripes, white waistcoats and white jackets bound with blue. As a girl of sixteen, she helped to make the first flag, a task completed by several ladies who worked through the night before the match. The material arrived late, and to save time, the sewers employed needle-threaders. The *Blackburn Standard*, of 23 August 1855, said 'the handsome red cross banner (kindly lent by the Cricketers' Club) floated from the church steeple on the day of the Sunday School procession'.

No details of the first match have survived, but it would not be unreasonable to suppose that it was played against the Newhallhey club, which had been formed in 1850 or 1851 by the Hardmans, who ran the large woollen mill there. A match against this club gave Haslingden its first mention in the Press. The *Preston Guardian*, of 17 June 1854, noted:

> On Saturday last a match was played between the first eleven of Haslingden and the second eleven of Rawtenstall on the ground of the latter. Haslingden first innings 36, second innings 77, Rawtenstall first innings 77, second innings 41 for five wickets.

William Rawlinson, one the first members, said in later life:

> The crease [at Bentgate] was about twenty yards by forty yards. All the rest of the field was mowing grass, and if a player could not find a ball played among it before six had been run, he called out, 'Lost ball!' and six runs were credited for the hit. The walls round the field were so low that Richard Hardman, of Cliff Tower, often jumped his horse over to watch a match. The tent, which stood at the top end, was about the size of a hencote.

A marked improvement in 1856 can be put down to the 'tuition of a professional gentleman engaged for the purpose, for some time'; and as the *Blackburn Standard* noted on 24 September:

> The Haslingden club has shown itself in its 'true colours' this year, not having lost a single match; and by study and persevering practice, bids fair to stand high amongst clubs in the neighbourhood.

A home game against Lowerhouse, said the *Preston Guardian* of 5 July, 'drew a large concourse of spectators, amongst whom were several of the fair sex'. In the two-innings match, Haslingden scored 64 and 47, and Lowerhouse 46 and 36. John Ormerod, who made 19 and 15, was the only Haslingden batsman to reach double figures. 'The underhand bowling of Mr Booth caused destructive work.' He took four wickets in the second innings.

As a skill, bowling was less regarded than batting; and the fact that the Haslingden players took it in turn, suggests it was a chore better undertaken at practice by working men or a professional, In 1864, Haslingden engaged Dan Rowland, of Bury, who received ten shillings for putting in three days a week. He was probably the player, who had been recruited by Bacup during the previous season and who was described by the *Bury Guardian*, of 13 June 1863, as 'a gentleman to instruct members in this manly and invigorating old English game'.

> He will be on the ground early in the day and will bowl to any member, who has the time to go and practise, until dusk.

In 1861, when Haslingden refused to allow artisans to play in matches, John Duckworth, aged seventeen and a future champion athlete, formed a breakaway club, which played for five seasons on

Laund Hey, at 1,100 feet above sea level, one of the highest arenas in the country. Enough young mountaineers joined the club to enable it to field two elevens, among them T. K. and David Whitehead of the Rawtenstall cotton family and sixteen-year-old William Rawlinson, who was later to make a name for himself at Bentgate.

Laund Hey won seven of the eleven matches in played in 1863, the most satisfying being the defeat of the Bentgate club by two runs. Other victories were against Lowerhouse (twice), Stacksteads Albion, Water and Lytham. Another game in that season was played at Longholme against '22 gentlemen of Rawtenstall', 'for the purpose', said the *Bacup and Rossendale News*, 'of promoting an interest in the game ... and ultimately causing the formation of a club at Rawtenstall'.

What led to the winding up of the Laund Hey club is not known, but there was a change of heart at Bentgate and by 1865, score sheets show that working men were outnumbering the gentleman, though a rule introduced in the following season warned that 'any member found either during practice or during matches playing in clogs be fined 2s. 6d.'

During the 1860s, the club began to charge for admission to games, but with due regard for the feelings of the class-conscious, divided the ground into upper and lower halves, the former being twice as costly to enter as the latter. Segregation was achieved in 1866 by erecting large boards, and to discourage people from looking over the low walls, the club put up long strips of canvas. When this not deter the Peeping Toms, the club raised the height of the wall at the lower end 'for 80 yards or thereabouts'.

The first mowing machine arrived in 1871, replacing a flock of geese and depriving small boys of the coppers they earned from collecting the droppings in baskets on the morning of match days. Professionals with county experience were engaged and new fixtures arranged with opponents as far off as Poulton-le-Fylde, but the 'Derby' games against Bacup were the highlights of the sporting year.

During the 1870s and '80s, cricket drew spectators in their hundreds to the Bentgate and Lanehead grounds. Not all were connoisseurs of the game. Some, by all accounts, had only a passing acquaintance with the game, but the prospect of an exciting spectacle, victory for one's own team and the humiliation of a vast horde of 'foreigners', had irresistible appeal.

Haslingden and Bacup had all the clannishness of independent small communities, and though many of the watchers were thoroughly biased, they were proud members of lively, participating societies. The progress of the cricket clubs was followed with the greatest interest; success bolstered local pride and brought public support, which turned into near fanaticism when 'Derby' days came round. A report by the *Bacup and Rossendale Times*, in 1878 catches the spirit of the times:

> The 1.25 train from Bacup was crowded to suffocation 'wi chaps beawnd to see th' cricketers!' Arrived at Rawtenstall, the usual custom of passing out of the station by the platform, and delivering up the tickets, was wholly ignored. Walls were scaled in all directions by the more adventurous and eager spirits and every available outlet was taken advantage of to 'get ahead'; and regardless of shouting officials and warnings from the station-master, the living tide poured forth, some onto the Haslingden road, but the majority onto the beaten track leading past Newhallhey Mill, which is said to be the shorter way to Bentgate.

The *Bacup Times* regretted that the 'bitter rivalry' between the two clubs, which was 'attended with deplorable ill spirit and ungovernable excitement on the part of the spectators'. Some games drew crowds of more than 4,000 and rowdyism declined as the years went by.

Haslingden began to play against Ramsbottom in 1883 and Rawtenstall three years later. Other opponents included Oldham, Skipton, Heywood, Rochdale, Padiham, Little Lever, Warrington, Huddersfield, Leeds and Manchester at Old Trafford.

When the Newhallhey club folded in 1861, cricket languished in Rawtenstall, and it was not until 1886 that the old rivalry resumed. A club was formed at Reedsholme in the late '60s, but having no ground, the players often walked miles to matches. No pads or gloves were used and the most important fielder was the 'long stop', wrote W. H. Hamer in his *History of the Rawtenstall Cricket Club*. When a field became available at Higher Constable Lee, the name was changed to Crawshawbooth, where the teams played until moving to Bacup

Road in 1886. 'A large and fashionable assemblage ... graced by the presence of ladies from the leading families in the district' watched the club beat Haslingden in their first encounter on the new ground, but having lost by 178 runs against their other neighbour, they were said by the *Times* to be 'in no department worthy to compete with an old-established well-tried XI such as Bacup can put in the field'. In 1892, the Haslingden *v.* Rawtenstall matches were, in the opinion of the *Rossendale Echo*, 'the Derby Day of all Derby days' and it commented:

> It becomes hard to find a new phrase sufficiently suggestive of the importance in local cricket circles – and the wide interest taken in outside cricket circles – in this match. There is no doubt that many persons who know nothing about cricket, who don't care a rap which team wins the day, now feel a lively interest in the annual encounter between Haslingden and Rawtenstall, especially, according to some 'would-be prophets', the credit and reputation of the dwellers therein are at stake ... The betting which takes place is simply lamentable. This spirit of backing up one's options by wagers is fast becoming the curse of all our national sports and is sapping all truly good love from our games. Individuals who profess never to bet and lift up their hands in pious indignation at the gambling spirit of the age, have been known to speculate a cigar on Haslingden or Rawtenstall.

There was great rejoicing in Haslingden in August, 1887, when the club won the Lancashire Cricket Association Amateur Cup in a knock-out competition begun three years earlier. Having beaten Accrington, Ordsall Hall and Bacup (at Lanehead before 'a vast concourse of spectators'), they met Church at Alexandra Meadows, Blackburn, in a two-innings match over three days. Church, who had soundly beaten Haslingden on the previous two Saturdays, were the firm favourites. 'Haslingden's chances of winning, declared the *Rossendale Free Press* on the first day of the match, 'appear to have descended below zero', and the 2,000 spectators must have thought so too as Church made 271 in their first innings. The last pair added 67 and no man was bowled. Haslingden then scored 231 and dismissed Church for 133. Haslingden achieved victory by scoring 181 for 5.

The team returned home [said the *Free Press*] in a waggonette drawn by six horses and were met at the top of Station Brow by the Rifle Band, who led the victors on their triumphant march to the strains of 'Rule Britannia'. Their arrival was the signal for a scene of the wildest excitement, the streets being lined with people waiting to give them a hearty welcome; and on the appearance of the waggonette, the welkin rang with the cheers of the assembled crowd. The team drove to the Commercial Inn, where the remainder of the evening was spent in joviality. The band stayed in the vicinity of the Commercial and rendered several selections of music. The streets presented a lively scene during the night, everyone being highly delighted with the success of the team.

League cricket began in 1891 and Haslingden waited until 1900 to be champions of the Lancashire League, thanks to a great extent to their professional Jack Usher, who took 143 wickets at only 6.93 each. Haslingden and Church ended the season with equal points and in a repeat of the Amateur Cup final, took part in two-innings play-off on Saturday and Monday. Accrington was the neutral ground. The game, which began at one o'clock, attracted 8,499 spectators on the first day. 'Factory people' reported the *Haslingden Gazette*, 'asked to be paid at twelve o'clock so they could get to the Accrington ground'.

Trams were run every few minutes. They were 'express trams' and it was distinctly refreshing to hear the guards call, 'First stop, Accrington'. They were all heavily laden. A good many people travelled by train and others by waggonette. Almost all Haslingden people who know anything about cricket attended the match.

Batting first, Haslingden made 162, George Parker scoring 74 and being rewarded with a collection of £12 17s. – 'many a man's weekly wage earned in a few seconds,' wrote the *Gazette* reporter. Church replied with 120, and Haslingden began their second innings on Monday after a very wet morning before 8,131 spectators. They reached 158 and dismissed Church for 84, Parker taking 6 for 37.

'The Haslingden team drove from the ground in a handsome stage coach drawn by six horses,' said the *Gazette*.

W. Warburton, the captain, seated at the front, took charge of the cup. The coach was followed by a large waggonette drawn by four horses, containing members of the committee and a few others. Then came a conveyance with some enthusiastic lady followers of the team, who have been absent from very matches this season ... There were numerous other waggonettes containing Haslingden people of all grades, and as Haslingden was approached the number increased ... Through the cheering crowd they drove on to Baxenden, the enthusiasm being sustained all the way. On this part of the journey, the procession was joined by Mr Jack Cordingley on his motor car and by numerous cyclists, ladies and gentlemen. A large assemblage of people awaited the arrival of the team and their train at the bottom of Hudrake, where the Haslingden Temperance Band was waiting. A short stoppage was made here to enable the procession to be formed in order, and numerous improvised torches and lanterns to be lighted. Then the triumphant cavalcade entered Haslingden proper to the strains of 'See the Conquering Hero Comes', which strains were, however, deadened by the cheers and ejaculations of the people along the route. Opposite the newspaper shop of Mr Dobson, an old supporter, fireworks were being let off. The sight was, however, at the junction of Manchester-road and Dearden-gate, near the Commercial Hotel. It seemed as though every man, woman and child of Haslingden had turned out and centred here. Looking from the waggonettes, one saw a perfect sea of upturned faces – all laughing, cheering, shouting. Some thousands of people must have been assembled.

In his 'Jottings' column, the reporter, A. J. Chappell, commented:

> The whole town on Monday was swept by enthusiasm as by a tornado. There may have been as big and demonstrative crowds as there were then, but never, I should say, have there been crowds as big and so united in the object in view.

Unmown and steeply sloping meadows were gratefully used by the teams that sprang up in all parts of the district, but even these 'arenas' must have seemed exceedingly well-appointed to the young cricketers who flocked in 1877 to what a writer in the local press laughingly described as 'one of Bacup's recreation grounds'. Were games ever played under more dangerously picturesque conditions than those which took place in a quarry, where an artificial plateau formed by the excavations provided space for a pitch, but not for an 'outfield'?

Large flat stones set up edgeways served as wickets on the narrow stretch of level bare rock, around which the fielders 'were placed out in a marvellous manner'. Some perched on top of crane beams, twenty or thirty feet from the bottom of the quarry; others took up their positions in hollows in the workings or 'down at the bottom among the hewn and uncut boulders left about on all sides'.

> The 'wicket plateau' terminates at one end in a narrow road formed over an arch-bridge under which a cart track rubs into the quarry; and on the bridge – not more than two yards wide and *minus* rails or protection of any kind – long stop essayed to save the byes.

Notwithstanding all these disadvantages, the writer noted, 'the cricket was enjoyed with a zest equal to, if not surpassing, that evinced by the Bacup First XI at Lanehead'.

> It mattered not that long stop occasionally found his way backwards over the edge of the bridge, or that square leg toppled off the crane beam in his endeavours to catch a 'skier'. There were plenty ready and willing to fill in the dangerous positions so awkwardly vacated, and after the short cessation of play to ascertain that no limbs were broken – and marvellous to say, none to my knowledge ever was – the game was resumed with unabated ardour until darkness rendered it not only dangerous, but utterly impossible to go on longer.

Night after night, the writer concluded, the quarry swarmed with boys of all ages and sizes, 'and watching them, I have spent many pleasing hours'.

Chapter 28

THE HALLELUJAH PIG

ROSSENDALE PEOPLE DELIGHTED in making their own pastimes, and, as we have seen, they were devoted church-goers, successful co-operators and keen sportsmen and music lovers. They also formed clubs and societies to satisfy an impressive variety of interests. At the same time, the Valley's prosperous reputation and the coming of the railway attracted a growing number of lecturers, educationists and entertainers; so that by the end of the century the public had a wide choice of fare on most nights of the week. This chapter records events in Haslingden.

From the *Preston Guardian*, of 4 June 1853, we learn of early arrivals.

> On Wednesday last, Mr Cooke's equestrian performers, accompanied by his train of elephants, reindeer, ostriches &c, passed through the principal streets of Haslingden in procession, and attracted considerable attention. Such a magnificent procession has not been before witnessed in this town. A large tent was erected in a meadow adjoining the [King Street] Methodist Chapel.

Religious rivalry made news in March, 1883, when 'the Salvation Army made its first appearance in Haslingden in opposition to the Christian Army'.

> During the day [reported the *Bury Times*] the streets were crowded with people to see the 'grand parades' of the rival armies. The Salvationists were first to gain possession of the 'Big Lamp' in the Market Place, and while they were engaged singing a hymn, the captain accompanying on his cornet, the members of the Christian Army marched up to the Market Place playing tambourines, concertinas, fiddles &, and paraded through the people around the Salvationists.

A visit to Haslingden by the 'Sheffield Hallelujah Band' in 1866, drew large congregations to the Town Hall, 'many attending out of mere curiosity,' said the *Bury Times*, of 17 November, 1866.

> This society, [it went on] is composed of a truly strange 'band' – reformed drunkards, converted thieves, race runners, dog and prize fighters – all of whom, having turned from 'the error of their ways', now exhort others to follow their good example.

Major David Halstead attended the meetings as a boy and set down his recollections,

> A noted Haslingden character of the 1860s was Henry Taylor, known to the majority as 'Owd Blue Tail'. During the American Civil War he was appointed watchman over the large stock of coal kept by the local Relief Committee and provided with a uniform – a bright, brass-buttoned coat and cord knee-breeches with long blue ribbons. The ribbons should have been knotted, but they were usually untied and waved in the breeze: hence the nickname.

> At one time he was a very heavy beer drinker, and spent much of his time in the tap-rooms of local beershops, and so neglected his home life very much. He was one of the many converts to the 'Hallelujah Band', who were prominent in Haslingden in my early days.

> This was a society of religious enthusiasts, undenominational and all of the working class, who met at the Big Lamp and later held meetings in the Town Hall, all of which were a source of joy

to us, as their hymns were sung to the tunes popular during the Cotton Famine. These were old nigger melodies of the slaves of the cotton plantations – 'Glory, Glory, Hallelujah', 'Kingdom Coming' and many others; and they were sung with a heartiness equal to the Christy Minstrels, many troupes of which were travelling the country, some of the performers having been slaves.

Another attraction came from the speeches or confessions of some of the converts, who described in the most lurid language the incidents of their past life. Reformed gaol-birds described their prison life, their experience on the 'everlasting staircase' (the tread mill) – how many steps to the minute – and at that time we could have recounted every incident of a prisoner's day from his early rising to his being locked in his cell at the close of the day's work.

An old poacher would tell us all the tricks of his profession, of the many encounters with gamekeepers or police and how he disposed of hares, rabbits and other game – and even mentioned some of his customers. Stories of wife-beating, the pawning of household goods to obtain drink, robberies committed and many other incidents were described most graphically.

One evening there was a special treat for us. Among others, Blue Tail was announced to give the record of his life.

Billy Lee was called upon for an opening address, but after a few minutes he suddenly halted. Words failed to come and a painful silence ensued. He had entirely lost the thread of his discourse, so after a time he burst out into singing 'I'm a Pilgrim Going Home'.

One after another men told horrible stories of their past life, encouraged by their friends with such calls as 'Go it, owd bird!' 'Glory Hallelujah!' and other interjections.

Then 'Owd Blue Tail' was called upon and received a most encouraging round of applause. He began by drawing attention to the blessings and comforts of a home from which drink was absent; how since he reformed he had been able to live in comfort, save money and furnish a house; how he spent his nights at the fireside with his wife, instead of in a tap-room as formerly; how at that moment a big fat pig belonging to him was hanging in the shop of 'Dick Butcher', decked out with blue ribbons and bearing the label 'Hallelujah pig'; how he hoped this would be cut up and sold during the approaching week, and he hoped everyone present would buy a bit.

Hearty applause encouraged him to begin to describe his life prior to his joining the 'Hallelujah Band', but here our hero out-Heroded Herod. He described the many scenes in such vivid detail as to shock everybody.

He finished by telling how 'last Belle Vue Monday' he chalked up thirty two pints at Owd Ned Barnes's , all of which he 'supped hissel', and he never thrat [treated] nobody because nobody thrat him'; then how he 'returned home at midneet, dragged t' wife eawt o' bed wi' yers ov her yead, torned her eawt o' th' heause i' her shift un' locked do'r on her' – and this was recounted with many horrible details.

Women screamed, men rose in anger, threats to murder him, calls to hang him, appeals from the audience to throw him from the platform – 'Send him to Botany Bay!' 'Fotch th' police!' Pandemonium reigned for some time, and if some of the women could have reached poor old Blue Tail, he would have been torn to pieces.

When the tumult was at its height, the big, burly figure of Police Sergeant Shaw appeared in the doorway and the disturbance subsided.

A more subdued atmosphere prevailed when Edwin Waugh, the Lancashire dialect writer, gave a series of Penny Readings in the

Haslingden Town Hall in 1867. 'Many people were unable to gain admission', said the *Blackburn Chronicle* in November. The Mechanics Institution sponsored the visits and engaged the Local Rifle Volunteers' Band to play selections. Mr James Lord performed a cornet solo 'in a very creditable manner'.

In September, 1873, 'Professor Smalley, the great mesmerist', hypnotised 'a goodly number of townspeople' when he appeared at Haslingden Public Hall. Binns, the ex-Hangman 'pitched his tent behind the New Inn, Haslingden, in September, 1873, 'and with a dummy figure performed mimic executions. He also shewed relics of certain murderers he had executed.'

The May Fair brought entertainment unavailable in the town, that in 1867 offering, in the words of the *Bury Guardian*, 'amusements ranging from a large circus to a peep show.'

> There were two sets of hobby horses, one propelled by steam power and the other by manual labour, but the juveniles preferred making circular journeys by steam. There were a couple of shooting galleries; swing boats and no end of nut and gingerbread stalls with pop guns for the amusement of the youngsters. Half a dozen caravans were said to contain all sorts of nondescript animals from the vasty deep and unknown regions. Manley's Circus has given two performances daily.

For the more scientifically-minded, the Horticultural and Botanic Society, in 1859, discussed 'The gooseberry caterpillar, its natural history and the best means to be used in destroying it'. A celery exhibition was held in the Railway Hotel in 1876 – fifty exhibitors; first prize a brass pan and £1 – and two years later, the Haslingden Society of Canary Fanciers staged a singing competition in the Warners Arms, when many people were unable to gain admission. A bird which sang for 371 seconds earned a gold hoop for its owner.

Chapter 29

A MEMORABLE TRIP

WHEN RAILWAYS REACHED ROSSENDALE in the 1840s, people were quick to widen their horizons by patronising the cheap trips the East Lancashire Company was happy to provide. Hundreds of people, who did not mind sitting in third-class carriages, or, to be more precise, roofless, unlit trucks with wooden seats, endured the discomfort of a long journey in order to visit places which had previously been well beyond their reach. The first trip from Helmshore and Haslingden to Liverpool, took six hours, but the novelty outweighed the drawbacks.

'On Saturday last, soon after daybreak,' said the *Blackburn Standard*, of 6 June 1849, 'many of the most active inhabitants were to be seen running backwards and forwards to call their more sleepy neighbours up, in order that they might not be late for the train'.

> At five o'clock, both the Helmshore and Haslingden stations were thronged with lads and lasses in their 'very best', and there appeared to be a good sprinkling of men and women of more sober age. The book-keeper at the Haslingden station, who unfortunately for him, slept in the office during the night, was 'rattled up' at half past three o'clock in the morning by eager people wanting tickets. The Helmshore party consisted of a large number of workpeople in the employ of Messrs. W. & R. Turner, the extensive merchants at Helmshore, who came up to Haslingden in a long train of carriages drawn bt three splendid engines at about seven o'clock.

They had an excellent band of music with them, the performers being workmen in the employ of Messrs. Turner.

At the Haslingden station, the workpeople of Messrs. Dean and Cronkshaw were in attendance and anxiously awaiting the Helmshore train; and when it was descried in the distance, a general cry of 'It's coming, lads' was raised, and the train shortly after reached the station, where a truly busy scene ensued,

A number of empty carriages had been attached to the train for the Haslingden party. These were soon filled without the least accident, and after some hearty cheers at starting, the train conveying the merry expectant parties was soon out of sight.

Not a single accident happened during the day. On the return of the party, the police were in attendance to facilitate the careful emptying of the carriages.

Chapter 30

New heights

As the nineteenth century progressed, the country grew accustomed to Rossendale people moving up in the world, but it came as a great delight in 1876, when a twenty one-years-old high jumper from the Valley became the first man in history to clear six feet. Marshall Brooks, second son of Thomas Brooks (the 1st Baron Crawshaw in 1892) was a student at Brasenose College, Oxford, where he used his own unique method to enter the record books.

Brooks became interested in athletics while at Rugby School, winning both the high jump (5ft 3in) and the long jump (20ft 3in) in 1873. Rugby union football was another passion; he played as a full back for Oxford throughout his stay and was in the England side against Scotland in 1874. During the same year he cleared 5ft 10in at the Inter-Varsity Sports and three days, later, 30 March, at the Amateur Athletics Association meeting, he achieved 5ft 11in to set a world record and become English champion.

Brooks approached the bar at little more than a walk and then sprang cat-like with his legs tucked in front of him. This allowed his body to pivot back, and when it seemed that he would hit the bar, he would jerk forward to clear the height and land on his toes.

A leg injury restricted Brooks's progress in 1875, but in the following year, which saw him elected as President of the Oxford University Athletic Club, he reached 5ft 11¼in while training. A large crowd gathered at Marston, near Oxford, on 17 March to see what the young man would do next. He did not disappoint the watchers, making history by clearing 6ft 0⅛in. Some 18 days later, and despite hostile weather – 'a stormy and bleak wind accompanied by snow,' according to *The Times* – another big crowd went to the Oxford University Athletic Sports and waited until 4pm before a start could be made. The high jump was staged on cinders and Brooks, having beaten his rivals, asked for the bar to be raised to 5ft 10in. He cleared it at the second attempt and then tried for 6ft. Twice he nudged off the bar with his elbow, but as tension rose, he then cleared 6ft 1in, 'the highest jump known to have been completed by either professional or amateur,' said *The Times*.

In the following month more than 15,000 spectators, many attracted by the feats of the Crawshawbooth prodigy, flocked to the annual contest between Oxford and Cambridge Universities. After eliminating his rivals, Brooks had the bar raised to a record 6ft 2½in, making it level with the top hats of the men who lifted it. To thunderous applause, Brooks made a perfect jump and landed on his toes before walking back under the lath. He had achieved fame 'without even troubling to remove his hat'. Brooks's mark was not surpassed until 1887 and his varsity record stood for 72 years.

From Haslingden came three other champions, James E. ('Choppy') Warburton, John Duckworth and G. W. Renshaw, who honed their skills when members of the town's Athletic Club, which was formed in 1868. Warburton (1843–1897) was the leading long-distance runner of his day and the English Amateur Champion in 1878. He won more than 700 trophies, 511 before he turned professional in 1880.

'As a boy at Hutch Bank Mill,' he told a *Sporting Chronicle* representative in 1894, 'I often had to go to Helmshore to ask the stationmaster to send an engine to Grane Road Sidings, when wagons loaded with cloth were ready to be taken away'.

> I used to run in the six-foot by the locomotive and try to race it from Helmshore. That is how I found out I could run. One day my master, Mr Duckworth [the athlete] saw me on the line and made

a match for me. I came into prominence right away, for I believe I was made for a runner.

In later life Warburton achieved notoriety, especially in France, when he used drugs – they were not illegal in those days – to enhance the performance of racing cyclists. With a touch of showmanship, he would produce his 'Little Black Bottle' for his protégées to drink. Its secret contents certainly appeared to help them win races, but at great cost to the riders; and when some of them became disoriented, Warburton was banned from the sport. He died in London of a heart attack, the only Haslingden man to have been drawn by a famous artist. He appears in a poster by Henri de Toulouse-Lautrec that was commissioned by a firm of bicycle chain makers.

Duckworth, who brought Warburton into sport, was a noted sprinter and jumper, becoming all-round champion of England in 1867. Renshaw, in 1885, was the country's amateur champion gymnast.

The formation of an Athletic Club in 1868 nurtured these and other men, who competed on the ground alongside Helmshore Road and above Deansgrave. The annual sports in 1869 attracted 8,000 spectators, including 'a number of fashionably-dressed ladies and gentlemen'. Pole leaping, running, performances on the horizontal bars, trotting matches and velocipede racing delighted the watchers.

The town's football club, which was formed in 1876, played both the Association game and Rugby Union for six seasons, after which the players gave up rugby, because, it was said, their prowess was such that no other team would take them on.

Index

Accrington 86
Acre Mill 12
American Civil War 18
Athletic News 113

Bacup 3, 10, 15, 51, 61, 68, 74, 77, 78, 80, 86, 90, 93–95, 101, 102, 110, 123
Bacup and Wardle Commercial Company 7, 8, 12
Bacup Choral Society 88, 91
Bacup Co-operative Society 14, 16
Bacup Cricket Club 117
Bacup Mechanics' Institution 19, 72, 74, 88
Bacup Natural History Society 68
Bacup Orchestral Society 87, 90
Bacup Sick Nursing Society 93
Balladenbrook 20
Barlow, James (illicit whisky spinner) 46
Barnes, Richard (tricycle maker) 86
Baxenden 71, 86
Belle Vue, Manchester 96, 97, 100, 102
Bentley House Farm 35
Binns, Batholomew (hangman) 128
Binns, Dr John 13
Blackburn Rovers 114
Blue Ribbon Army 48, 81
Bolton Wanderers 111
Borwick, Leonard (pianist) 92
Bottesini, Giovanni (musician) 87, 88
Broadclough 111
Broadclough Band 97
Bromoley, William (illicit whisky distiller) 45
Brooks, Marshall (high jumper) 131
Brooks, Thomas (industrialist) 4, 131

Brooks, William (industrialist) 66, 69
Brown, Dr. 74
Buckley, Baxter (pianist) 90
Burnley Football Club 111
'Bury Bob' (Robert Hamer) 49–51

Calf Hey Mill 43
Carl Rosa Opera Co. 73
Canary singing 128
Cawl Terrace Co-operative Society 14
Celery exhibition 128
Chappell, A. J. (journalist) 122
Chartists 8
Church Cricket Club 120, 121
Cloughfold 5
Cloughfold Football Club 114
Cobden, Richard 13
Cordingley, Jack (motorist) 122
Cotton Famine 13, 18, 99, 126
Coventry 10
Crawshawbooth 18, 66
Crawshawbooth Co-operative Hall 4, 69
Crawshawbooth Cricket Club 119
Crawshawbooth Literary and Mechanics' Institution 60
Crawshawbooth Wesleyan School 69
Crystal Palace 3, 101, 103, 105, 109

Dark Lane football ground 114
Davitt, Michael 25
Dean Layrocks 91
Disraeli, Benjamin 1
D'Oyly Carte Operatic Company 92

Duckworth, John (businessman and athlete) 132
Duke of Edinburgh (balloon) 81

East Lancashire Railway Company 129
Edgesideholme Mill 19
Edgworth 35, 67
Edgworth Football Club 67
Edenfield 45, 81, 90
Ellis, George (brass bandsman) 97
English Lyric Opera and Burlesque Company 89
Entwistle, Alice (illicit whisky distiller) 47
Ewood Bridge 68

Fair, Thomas (estate manager) 54
Farholme Mill 9
Ferny Bank Farm 46, 47
Flash Mills 68
Flaxmoss House 68
Fletcher, Percy (composer) 107, 108

Gaghills 29, 31
Glen Bottom Fair 86
Goodshaw Band 109
Goodshawfold 109
Grane Road sidings 79
Green, George (balloonist) 81

Hacking, Richard (engineer) 7
Hallé, Sir Charles 88, 89, 91
Halstead, David (local historian) 43, 125
Hare Clough 46
Hargreaves, D. (watchmaker) 71
Hagreaves, Elijah (cotton manufacturer) 54, 59, 60
Hargreaves, Richard (illicit whiskey distiller) 35, 44
Hargreaves Street Mill 23, 24

Haslingden 2, 48, 64, 65, 67, 70, 73, 87, 90
Haslingden Commercial Company 23, 24
Haslingden Cotton Weaving and Spinning Company 12
Haslingden Co-operative Relief Committee 13
Haslingden Cricket Club 115–23
Haslingden Horticultural and Botanical Society 128
Haslingden Industrial Co-operative Society 15, 68
Haslingden May Fair 128
Haslingden Orchestral Society 90
Haslingden Poor Law Union 3
Haslingden Public Hall 48
Haslingden Society of Canary Fanciers 128
Haslingden Technical Instruction Committee 64
Haslingden Town Hall 125, 128
Haworth, Alice 43
Haworth, George (cotton manufacturer) 18
Haworth, Henry (illicit whisky distiller) 46
Haworth, Jonathan (illicit whisky distiller) 36
Heald Sunday School 112
Heath, Ellis (Excise officer) 36, 38, 44
Heap, Moses (diarist) 2
Helmshore 46, 53, 58, 68, 90
Holbrooke, Joseph (composer) 108–9
Holden & Co. (tea merchants) 68
Hollows, Charles (choirmaster) 91
Holman, Henry (schools inspector) 64, 65
Holt Mill 19
Hoyle, J. Craven (cotton manufacturer) 26, 74

Hoyle, Edward (mill owner) 26, 108
Hoyle, Isaac (mill owner) 26
Hugh Mill 53
Hunter, Frank (accountant) 7
Hutch Bank Mill 76, 132

Ilex Mill 21
Irwell Springs Band 3, 100
Irwell Springs Football Club 111, 114
Irwell Springs Dyeworks 70, 112
Irwell Vale 68
Isles, J. H. (impresario) 101, 103

Jarvis, Police Superintendent Richard 18–19, 22
Jones, Benjamin (author) 23
Josuha Hoyle & Company 26

Kay Street Baptist Chapel 67

Lancashire Cricket Association 120
Lancashire Rifle Volunteers 97, 98, 99
Lancashire Cup 111, 114
Laneside Mill 23
Laund Hey Cricket Club 118
Leach, Isaac (brass bandsman) 97
Lee Mill 20, 85
Leoncavallo, Ruggero (composer) 106–7
Liverpool 129
Loveclough Print Works 67
Lowerhouse Cricket Club 117

Maden, John (cotton manufacturer) 20
Maden, J. H. (politician) 4, 93, 104
Maden, Mrs J. H. 92, 93
Magnetic Telegraph Company 72
Marston 131
Marx, Karl 12
Mather, Sir William (industrialist) 64, 65

Maxwell, James (architect) 55
Maxwell and Tuke 55
McLerie, S. (slipper manufacturer) 29
Melba, Dame Nellie 93
Mitchell, R. J. C. (felt manufacturer) 48
Morris, James (illicit whisky distiller) 38–41, 43
Morris, John 42
Morris, William Snr. 42
Morris, William, Jnr. 42
Mill, J. S. 13, 15–16
Muir, Angus (historian) 56, 59
Murphy, Thomas E. (anti-drink campaigner) 48, 51
Musbury 46
Munn, Rev. J. T. 99
Munn, Robert (cotton manufacturer) 19
Munn, Lt. Col. Robert (cotton manufacturer and musician) 88, 96, 98, 99

National Brass Band Championship 101, 105, 109
National Telephone Co. 74
New Inn, Haslingden 128
Newbigging, Thomas (local historian) 16
Newchurch 6
Newchurch Mechanics' Institution 19
Newchurch Spinning and Weaving Company 5
Newhallhey Cricket Club 26
Newhallhey Mill 26

Old Clough Mill 19
Old Factory, Grane 35
Oddfellows 2
Ordsall Hall Cricket Club 120
Ormerod, John (cricketer) 117
Osset 54
Oswaldtwistle 54
Oswestry Football Club 113
'Owd Blue Tail' 126, 127
Owen, Alex (brass bandsman) 106

Oxford University Athletic Club 131
Oxford University Athletic Sports 132

Paghouse Mill 71
Parker, George (cricketer) 121
Patrick, Captain (factory inspector) 9
Patterson brothers (inventors) 86
'Pattersons' Elephant' 86
Phonograph 92
Pike Law 38, 42
Porritt.W. J. (woollen manufacturer) 54, 58, 59
Priestley, L. J. (shopkeeper) 103, 105
Post Office Savings Bank 53
Preston, W. H. (magistrates' clerk) 34
Professor Smalley (mesmerist) 128

Queen's Hotel, Bacup 101
Queen's Hotel, Rawtenstall 68

Ramsbottom 79, 80
Ramsbottom Cricket Club 119
Rawlinson, William (cricketer) 116
Rawtenstall 17, 26, 51, 52, 66, 68, 70, 73, 80
Rawtenstall Co-operative Hall 15, 16, 50, 67, 88
Rawtenstall Co-operative Society 14, 15
Rawtenstall Cricket Club 116
Rawtenstall Football Club 114
Renshaw, G. W. (athlete) 133
Renton Football Club 113
Rimmer, William (brass bandsman) 101, 106
Rishton 54
Rising Bridge 74
Rochdale 11
Rossendale 1, 4, 8, 48, 113
Rossendale Charity Shield 112, 114

Rossendale Football Club 114
Rossendale Industrial Company 11
Rossendale Hunt 98
Rothwell, J. W. (slipper manufacturer) 29
Rowland, Dan (cricketer) 117
Royal Court Theatre, Bacup 92
Rye Hill 52, 67

Sadler, Windham William (balloonist) 81
Salisbury, Lord 73
Salvation Army 124
St Annes-on-Sea 54–60
St James's Church, Waterfoot 96
Shawforth 83
Sheffield Hallelujah Band 125
Shepherd, Abraham (band president) 105
Simpson, John (local historian) 42, 43
Sir J. C. Lee & Co. 67
Smith, G. A. (manufacturer) 68
Spring Holme Mill 20
Spring Mill, Dean 75
Stacksteads 9, 49
Stacksteads Albion Cricket Club 118
Stacksteads Co-operative Society 14
Stacksteads Mill 19
Stacksteads Philharmonic Society 90
Stacksteads WMC Football Club 114
Sullivan, Sir Arthur 101
Sunnybank Mill 56
Sutcliffe, J. S., 70
Sutcliffe, Wm. & Sons 68

Taylor, J. W. (football manager) 112
'Teetotal Samson' 52
Thistle Mount 99
Thorn Mill 18
Throstle Mill 20

Thwaites, Daniel (brewer and magistrate) 41
Townsend, Mrs J. (flag maker) 116
Trickett, Sir W. H. (slipper manufacturer) 28–33, 68
Trickett's Arcade, Waterfoot 68
Tupling, Dr G. H. (historian) 47
Tunstead Co-operative Society 16
Turner, W. & R. 129
Turton Football Club 114

Usher, Jack (cricketer) 121

Vale Mill 6
Victoria Mill 5

Warburton, J. E. ('Choppy') 132, 133
Warburton, W. (cricketer) 122
Ward, Mrs Humphrey (novelist) 78, 79
Waterfoot 15, 18, 28, 68, 73, 90, 96
Waterfoot Conservative Club 73
Waugh, Edwin (dialect writer) 127
Webb, Beatrice (Mrs Sidney Webb) 3, 61–63, 78
Westall, Benjamin (Excise officer) 35, 36, 45
Whelan, Captain (balloonist) 82
Whitaker Park Museum 90, 109
Whitehead, David (cotton manufacturer) 20, 21
Whitehead, J. W. (cotton manufacturer) 54, 56
Whitehead, Peter (cotton manufacturer) 20, 66
Whitewell Vale Agricultural Society 86
Whitworth Manufacturing Company 11
Wilcock, David (musician) 90
Workington Cup 109

Yate and Pickup Bank 44